CW00370272

critical skills
for tomorrow

Our future. It's in our hands

sub-editors:	Caroline Proud,
	Lesley Malachowski
production manager:	Lisa Robertson
design:	Halo Design
chief operating officer:	Andrew Main Wilson
chairman:	Miles Templeman

Published for the Institute of Directors and the Learning
and Skills Council by Director Publications Ltd
116 Pall Mall London SW1Y 5ED
Ⓣ 020 7766 8950 Ⓦ www.iod.com

The Institute of Directors, the Learning and Skills Council and
Director Publications Ltd accept no responsibility for the views
expressed by contributors to this publication. Readers should
consult their advisers before acting on any issue raised.

© Copyright April 2008 Director Publications Ltd
A CIP record for this book is available from the British Library
Printed and bound in Great Britain.

About the Learning and Skills Council

The Learning and Skills Council (LSC) is a publicly-funded organisation charged with building a dynamic and successful Further Education (FE) system for England, to give young people, adults and employers the high quality learning and skills they need for economic and social success.

We fund all learning for young people, aged 16–19 in colleges, schools and training providers, ensuring they have a full range of high-quality courses to choose from, so that they gain the skills and qualifications they need to progress into further learning, including Higher Education, and employment.

We also work alongside employers so that they can develop the skills of their employees. This helps ensure a positive platform for organisations to expand and supports the wider ambition and career progression of their staff.

We invest in adults to give them the skills they need for success in work and in life. For those not in work, we help them to get the training and support they need to get a good job and we are passionate advocates of the role of skills in supporting greater social mobility and social justice.

We are uniquely positioned to draw together information on skills and employment and our national, regional and local structures mean we know where skills gaps are located and how best to fill them. We use our expertise to advise and influence the activities of others so that, working together, we respond to the challenges that face us, improve investment in skills and training and help our country compete more successfully in a global economy.

CONTENTS

introduction
the need for collaboration _____ 5
Miles Templeman, Director General, IoD

foreword
enhancing the skills of your workforce _____ 7
Christopher N Banks CBE

1 the skills challenge _____ 9
Jessica Twentyman

2 meeting the challenge _____ 15
Peter Bartram

3 where do I start? _____ 24
Jessica Twentyman and Alison Coleman

4 training and the small business _____ 31
Laura Mazur and Alison Coleman

5 tomorrow's workforce _____ 41
Laura Mazur

6 sectors in the spotlight _____ 45
Jessica Twentyman and Alison Coleman

7 training for innovation _____ 53
Alison Coleman

8 the learning organisation _____ 58
Alison Coleman

9 return on training investment _____ 64
Alison Coleman

10 2020 vision _____ 71
Peter Bartram

Useful contacts _____ 77

Peter Bartram, Alison Coleman, Laura Mazur and Jessica Twentyman are independent business writers.

the need for collaboration

**Miles Templeman, Director General
Institute of Directors**

The skills gap. It's one of the biggest problems facing employers in every location across this country. A recent survey found that 90 per cent of our members believe that not only could the education system do more to prepare young people for work but that business should do more too. This means we need businesses and educators spending more time talking to each other, and working together, to bridge the skills gap.

It's about collaboration. Businesses need input from schools and colleges as to what they find most valuable. And schools and colleges need to know what business is looking for. This Guide has been designed to help businesses weave their way through each groups' needs.

It is designed to highlight clearer and more structured ways of working in partnership. There are a wide range of programmes detailed including the LSC's Train to Gain service, the Skills Pledge, Apprenticeships and Investors in People. These services all help employers maximise the potential of their employees, and their businesses, by providing a structural template through which they can solve their individual skills problems.

There are innovative and accessible ways to fill each skills gap. Many of our members comment on a lack of employability skills encompassing punctuality and teamwork to work ethic and creativity. They are vital to driving forward the knowledge economy and we must harness these skills if we are to remain competitive in the world market.

Apprenticeships are a logical and shrewd solution to this gap as employers are able to teach vital skills directly to staff, alongside the skills they need for that particular role from the start of their career.

This one example highlights how different suggestions put forward in this guide can enable employers and employees to work together to build the critical skills we need to be successful. Read on to discover how the services outlined can help your organisation achieve its business ambitions and close the skills gap.

enhancing the skills of your workforce

Christopher N Banks CBE
Chair Learning and Skills Council

Staff, the most valuable asset of any company, really can make or break your business. Expanding their skills is one of the most important investments you can make. And, rather than viewing it as a cost, let's embrace a culture where we can welcome the high return on investment it brings.

As our businesses increasingly compete in markets focused on higher added value products and services, the number of non-skilled jobs continues to fall. Over the next decade, almost every UK adult will need to acquire the equivalent of five good GCSEs and two thirds will need the equivalent of A-Levels.

At the LSC, we are working with our partners across government, business and education to improve knowledge of these increased demands and explain how we can take advantage of the opportunities this represents. After talking, and listening, to businesses, we have put in place a range of products and services to help you access training that will meet the skills requirements of your organisations, and your staff.

I am therefore delighted that we have worked with the IoD to produce this Directors Guide, which will provide you with all the information you need to enhance the skills of your workforce.

As the Guide will highlight, our key service Train to Gain, offers a single source of independent yet specific training advice to employers. Between April 2006 and December 2007, almost 70,000 employers used the service; and those who have, think it's great. The analysis provided by the Train to Gain skills brokers can help you identify hidden talent and skills gaps. And as you will read, companies that close their skills gaps see demonstrable benefits and financial returns.

The Guide also provides information on the highly popular and successful Apprenticeship programme, National Skills Academies and details of how you can make the Skills Pledge. More than 950 companies have already signed the pledge, making public their commitment to reviewing the training and skills needs of their workforce.

We know those leaders who invest in training are more likely to attract motivated staff, reduce absenteeism and improve staff retention. We hope this guide will inspire you to achieve this, safe in the knowledge you will get a return for your company, your staff and ultimately UK plc.

the skills challenge

Britain needs a skilled workforce at every level if it is to compete and succeed in a dynamic world economy. Jessica Twentyman reports

Think of Britain's skills crisis and you may think first of recent reports that many British people still lack a basic education.

There's little doubt that poor numeracy and literacy skills are costing UK businesses dearly – around £4.8bn annually, according to government figures. Every day, millions of people go to work without the basic skills they need to maximise their job potential. In England, 5.2 million adults of working age have literacy skills below Level 1 and would be unable to pass an English GCSE. For numeracy, the figures are even higher: 6.8 million adults have numeracy skills below Entry Level 3, broadly equivalent to the level expected of an 11 year old. And, a 2006 survey by the CBI suggested that one in three employers were having to give their staff remedial lessons in English and maths.

EXECUTIVE SUMMARY

- [ ] government figures put the cost of poor levels of literacy and numeracy among the workforce at £4.8bn a year
- [ ] the Leitch review of skills called for urgent action to tackle the problem of poor educational attainment
- [ ] the UK trails the US and mainland Europe in the productivity league
- [ ] many employers complain that graduate recruits lack team-working and communication skills

the importance of a skilled workforce

The former skills envoy Digby Jones has referred to the five million adults in the UK who are functionally illiterate as Britain's 'shameful and unspoken secret'. If more isn't done to raise standards, he has warned, the social and economic cost

THE LEITCH REVIEW: MAIN RECOMMENDATIONS

In 2004, the government commissioned Sandy Leitch to carry out an independent review of the UK's long-term skills needs. His final report, 'Prosperity for all in the global economy – world-class skills', published in December 2006, highlighted the challenges ahead and suggested proposals to make the UK world class by 2020:

- [ ] increase adult skills across all levels
- [ ] strengthen employer voice and better articulate employer views on skills by creating a new Commission for Employment and Skills
- [ ] increase employer engagement and investment in skills. Reform, re-license and empower Sector Skills Councils (SSC)
- [ ] deliver more economically valuable skills by only allowing public funding for vocational qualifications where the content has been approved by SSCs
- [ ] expand skills brokerage services for both small and large employers
- [ ] launch a new 'Pledge' for employers to voluntarily commit to train all eligible employees up to Level 2 in the workplace
- [ ] increase employer investment In Level 3 and 4 qualifications in the workplace. Extend Train to Gain to higher levels
- [ ] dramatically increase Apprenticeship volumes
- [ ] increase people's aspirations and awareness of the value of skills to them and their families
- [ ] create a new integrated employment and skills service, based upon existing structures, to increase sustainable employment and progression

of this unskilled adult population is likely to prove "fundamentally damaging to Britain's chance of winning in the 21st century".

Lord Leitch, the Scottish peer behind the 2006 skills review (see box above), agrees. His report says that to remain competitive, Britain will need a workforce educated to a minimum of Level 2 (the equivalent of five GCSE passes) by 2020.

knock-on effects

There's more to the skills problem than poor GCSE results, though. Much more. For a start, there's the knock-on effect of low educational attainment. Without Level 2, employees are unlikely to achieve the skills needed to enable businesses and UK plc to be competitive. Out of 30 OECD countries, the UK not only lies

17th on low skills, but also 20th on intermediate skills, and 11th on high skills.

The last biannual survey by the Association of Graduate Recruiters (January 2007) revealed a 15 per cent rise in the number of vacancies for graduates. Good

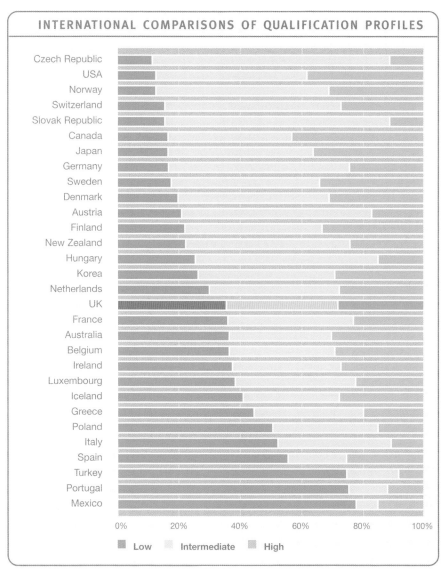

INTERNATIONAL COMPARISONS OF QUALIFICATION PROFILES

Base: Adult population aged 25-64.   Source: Education at a glance, OECD, 2006.

news for students? Not necessarily. There's more to this supply and demand problem than meets the eye.

The fact is that many employers are struggling to fill vacancies because the pool of graduates doesn't meet their requirements. Many employers surveyed by the AGR complained of "an inadequate supply of [graduate] applicants of sufficient calibre", with many lacking 'soft skills' such as team working and "communication plus verbal and numerical reasoning".

poor productivity levels

Anyone doubting that the skills gap is a serious problem for the British economy should consult the 2007 Sector Skills Almanac.

Produced by public body the former Sector Skills Development Agency (SSDA), the Almanac maps skills across 27 economic sectors. For 2007, it shows that, while the UK's employment rate is the fourth highest in Europe, its overall productivity levels are still 21 per cent behind the US and eight per cent lower than mainland Europe.

"The UK is starting from a position of disadvantage, and significant progress is required if we are to ensure a strong economy for the future," says Professor Mike Campbell, director of research and policy at the UK Commission for Employment and Skills. "There is a shortage of basic and employability skills, vocational and technical skills, and intermediate and higher level skills are more plentiful in the workforces of other countries," he says.

Accordingly, the UK's productivity level relative to its competitor countries is weak, says Professor Campbell. "The difference is stark, whether 'per hour' or 'per worker' measures of productivity are considered," he says. Naturally, the picture varies from sector to sector – but it doesn't take much investigation to see from the figures that, in 18 of the 27 sectors, European companies are more productive, and in 20, the US has an advantage.

According to the Almanac, UK companies are outperforming their US and EU counterparts by a considerable margin in only two sectors – mining and quarrying. By narrower margins, we are leading in food, drink and tobacco; publishing, printing and reproduction of recorded media; sales, maintenance and repair of motor vehicles; and an unwieldy category that groups together furniture, musical instruments, toys, jewellery and various other manufactured goods.

But we are comprehensively outshone in a number of crucial areas of business: textiles and their products; wood, paper and pulp; basic and fabricated metals; transport equipment; construction; retail; and financial services, to name a few.

The good news is that significant progress is being made in addressing the skills problem. Almost three-quarters (74 per cent) of the workforce now reach Level 2 – a 'major milestone', according to Chris Banks, chairman of the government-funded Learning and Skills Council (LSC).

long way to go

Compared with four years ago, over 1.14 million more adults are now qualified to Level 2. This is around 17.7 million people from a total economically active population of 23.7 million. But there is still a long way to go. As Banks says: "The flip side of the coin is that one-quarter of adults still need to be helped with their skills. Not only are they suffering as a result, but so are the companies that employ them."

It's in our hands.

Without training your staff, will your business have a bright future?

meeting the challenge

Peter Bartram looks at government initiatives to solve the skills problem and fulfil the training needs of business

The global economy is evolving rapidly, with falling barriers, new opportunities and emerging challenges. The jobs of yesterday will not be the jobs of tomorrow, and we all – government, business and individuals – need better skills than ever before.

It is currently estimated that skills gaps cost £165,000 for a typical <50 employee business every year. Good skills undeniably help build a good business. It's a message that more directors have started to take on board. But the big question is: how can a company train its staff in skills that will help them deliver better bottom-line performance?

David Lammy MP, parliamentary under secretary of state for skills, admits: "Employers have long complained with some justification

EXECUTIVE SUMMARY

- ☐ through the Train to Gain service more employees are reaching Level 2 and improving their skills at all levels, from basic literacy and numeracy to Level 3, plus training in leadership and management – thus providing the training solutions businesses really need

- ☐ the Skills for Business Network is working in partnership with higher education colleges

- ☐ the National Skills Academy Network is putting employers in the driving seat to set industry standards for delivering skills

- ☐ new Diplomas are helping prepare young people for the world of work

- ☐ the Get On campaign works with colleges, libraries and prisons to get adults to sign up for free literacy or numeracy courses in their local area

- ☐ Apprenticeships are being expanded to improve the skills of the nation (see chapter 5)

TRAIN TO GAIN: BROKERING A SOLUTION

The LSC's Train to Gain service aims to help businesses choose the most suitable training, enabling them to compete, and most importantly, to grow. It brings employers and independent, impartial and experienced skills brokers together. The role of the skills brokers is to identify skills gaps, offering suggestions as to the best way to provide training to plug those gaps, and in some cases, facilitate that training. Train to Gain skills brokers offer impartial and independent advice, match any training needs identified with training providers and ensure that training is delivered to meet business needs.

The key difference between Train to Gain and previous methods of business training is the service's flexibility, which makes it more responsive to a whole range of different businesses of all sizes and disciplines. Training and workplace skills advice is tailored to the distinctive requirements of each business and is made available at a time and place to suit them.

Train to Gain skills brokers review and analyse the employer's business to assess both current and future skills needs. This could include anything from first Level 2 and Level 3 and Skills for Life – like English for Speakers of Other Languages (ESOL). Skills brokers also provide employers with a range of skills advice, discussing anything from Apprenticeships and basic skills through to recruitment issues and higher level skills.

For example, a small high street retail business might be shown how to increase its profile online, or a mechanic could receive sales training in order to expand into selling car parts alongside the original business. A Train to Gain broker will also recommend the best funding options available to the business, and government funding may be available to organisations that are eligible under the service's guidelines.

Train to Gain is the government's flagship service to support employers in England, of all sizes and in all sectors, to improve the skills of their employees, unlock talent plus drive and improve business performance. Train to Gain is expanding to help even more businesses get the training they need to succeed and by continuing to improve the service, we will ensure that even more businesses benefit from access to high quality skills advice and support. Since launch, Train to Gain has helped almost 70,000 employers across the country to improve the skills levels of almost 330,000 employees.

David Woodward

that the education and training for their employees does not give them the knowledge and skills they need.

"This is something we are addressing and are determined to put right," Lammy adds: "Part of the government's solution is the Train to Gain service." Run by the Learning and Skills Council (LSC), this gives employers access to independent, impartial 'skills brokers' who help them identify skills gaps and plug them through training and development. (See box above.)

But can directors who join the programme be confident they'll get a return? The question is especially important for small and medium-sized companies, where budgets are often tight, and where employee time away from the job has to be justified with demonstrable benefits.

There's strong evidence that the answer's yes. Consider the case of Jennifer Allen, who was marketing account manager at the Hardy Group, an east London print company with six full-time staff and 25 freelance workers. In 2006, Allen went on a one-day project management course, sourced by a skills broker under the auspices of Train to Gain. Allen returned from the course brimming with new knowledge and ideas and has since been promoted to director.

Even more importantly, the company's turnover has leapt 44 per cent since it started training its staff. And Allen adds: "My bosses are saying that the training I did has allowed me to be promoted – and because of the new role I've developed as a result, the turnover is up."

Since that first course, training has become a regular part of staff development at the Hardy Group. For example, financial director David Douglas and sales director Ken Stanger attended a five-day management course – with a diploma at the end to recognise the new skills they'd acquired.

Another company that used a skills broker to find the courses needed was Yorkshire-based Crabtree Care Homes, which runs two homes and has 65 staff. Already some staff have completed NVQ Level 2 training in literacy and numeracy and others NVQ Level 2 training programmes in specialist subjects such as palliative care. Other employees have been on IT courses.

associated benefits

Andrew Crabtree, human resources manager of the company, says that one of the big benefits has been reduced staff turnover – down from 25 per cent a year to 15 per cent. "Train to Gain has played a large part in this reduction," he says. "Some people take the training and leave – and that is natural. But we have found there has been a significant response to the investment we've put in and, as a consequence, people have not felt the need to move on."

Gillen's, which runs six pubs and eight supermarkets in the Hartlepool area, is similarly positive about the pay back. Thanks to Train to Gain, most of its 300 staff have now had NVQ Level 2 training in customer care or retail; some have even gone on to Level 3. Leo Gillen, head of operations at the company, says: "The training has been a great benefit in raising staff morale. We have a relatively low staff turnover for our industry. The training works well in improving motivation. It gives staff a greater understanding of the job, which helps them to do it better."

Gillen adds: "The training should lead to increased profitability. It's difficult to say, but it should be a factor. If somebody is well motivated about the job, they are going to do it better and, in the long run, that is only a good thing."

A central element of the Train to Gain service and the current work of the LSC is employer-friendly training. In the past, as Lammy notes, many directors have complained that the training courses available haven't matched up to what businesses need.

In November 2007 Train to Gain was extended to provide sector-specific skills advice to businesses of all sizes. The expanded service will enable employers of all sizes, in all locations and across all sectors to take the future of their business into their hands through access to high quality training advice and support. In this way, it will play a key role in reaching out to the one in three businesses that still do not offer staff any training – and so will transform the nation's skills base, productivity and competitiveness between now and 2020.

get your own in-house training accredited

Employers that have already invested in their own top-quality training and development programmes, can now work with the Qualifications and Curriculum Authority (QCA) to have that training nationally recognised and accredited. This will give their training programmes the recognition they deserve, plus it gives employees a recognised qualification that they can take with them through their working lives.

To date three companies have been approved to award their own qualifications – McDonalds, Flybe and Network Rail – and a further 24 companies are getting specific qualifications accredited.

business/education partnerships

The Government's approach to skills and training is based on the principle of partnership between business and the education sector. A key body in all this is the Sector Skills Development Agency (SSDA), which is responsible for funding and promoting a new network of Sector Skills Councils (SSC). There are currently 25 councils covering a wide range of industry areas. They include Asset Skills, for those working in cleaning and facilities management, Improve, for those in food manufacture, and Skillfast UK, for clothing and footwear manufacture. All SSCs have the power to create new vocational qualifications or revise existing ones, based on employers' needs.

Together, the SSDA and SSC form the Skills for Business Network. "The phrase sums up what we're all about," says Professor Mike Campbell, director of development at the SSDA. The aim is make sure that business has a much greater say in the kind of training and qualifications that are on offer.

One sign of the seriousness of the new approach is the alliance between the Skills for Business Network and the Association of Colleges (AoC), the organisation that represents around 300 colleges in the UK. The alliance will make it easier for business to work with colleges to develop the training and qualifications they actually need, says Maggie Scott, director of learning and quality at the AoC.

Already, 14 new sector skill groups have been set up, bringing together both employers and colleges. Each is led by a college principal, and they are working to develop skills training ranging from writing and accrediting new qualifications to the development of foundation degrees and diplomas. The aim is to make all qualifications more relevant to business's needs. "It is making sure that the courses that are on offer are fit for purpose," says Scott.

Campbell cites the example of IT degrees. "The group looking at this felt that IT degrees on offer were technically fine, but the people who went through the courses lacked management skills," he says. "The group has worked with four universities to develop a new IT programme that combines the technical requirements of the IT industry with the development of management, interpersonal and relationship skills."

Bridgwater College in Somerset is another example of the education sector co-operating with business. It has worked with the south-west based luxury leather goods company Mulberry to develop a new Apprenticeship qualification, especially designed for the company's needs. (See case study, chapter 5, page 42.)

A further vehicle to make training more employer-friendly are the new National Skills Academies (NSAs). Lammy says: "Academies are also a key element in our drive to raise the skills levels of the UK workforce, which is so vital if we are to maintain our economic success and compete in the global markets of the future.

"They are unique, employer-led partnership organisations designed to give employers a much greater say say in influencing and developing the skills people need to boost productivity and improve competitiveness in their sector. They put employers firmly in the driving seat, and this means that the content and delivery of training is dynamic and responds quickly to changing sector needs. They are, therefore, in an ideal position to ensure the availability of high-quality training that fully meets their expectations."

widening the net

Local Employment Partnerships (LEPs), which were announced by Gordon Brown in March 2007 and are part of a range of initiatives handled by Jobcentre Plus, bring an additional group of job candidates into the 'skills' net. Up to 250,000 people who are in the labour market – but are in various ways overlooked – will be helped into work by 2010. Some of these will need training, but the 'deal' which employers sign up to is encouraging greater involvement and investment by them to ensure effective integration into their workforce. One benefit is likely to be better value from the investment in Train to Gain.

skills for employability

Results from the LSC's 2007 Impact of Learning on Employability research found that nearly four in ten (38 per cent) learners who were claiming workless benefits at the start of their FE course have worked since finishing their learning. In addition, one in three learners are currently in employment and not claiming workless benefits.

However, employment outcomes are less positive for learners with multiple disadvantages. That said, those with multiple disadvantages do benefit from a positive impact of learning in terms of improved communication skills, increased confidence and propensity to get involved in their communities.

The government has set some challenging targets to tackle the problem of the nation's skills shortage. For basic skills for life the government has asked that 2.25 million adults improve their basic skills by 2010 and 95 per cent of adults to be functionally literate (a minimum of Level 1) by 2020.

The Get On campaign encourages adults to call 0800 66 0800 and enrol on a free literacy or numeracy course in their local area. The adverts which for many years featured a nasty gremlin who brought to life the feelings of frustration, fear and isolation that adults with poor numeracy or literacy can face, have resulted in some impressive results. So far, 1,759,000 learners have achieved a first Skills for Life qualification.

In the business environment it is expected that by the end of 2010, over 500,000 learners will have achieved a first full Level 2 qualification through Train to Gain.

Yet while all this work may be encouraging, some employers are still questioning the basic employability of young people entering the workforce. "Employers have told us that existing qualifications may give students the professional and

QUALIFYING FOR A NEW START

Asher Walton from Leicester did not get on well academically at school, only achieving Ds and Es in her GCSEs. When she left school, Asher took a job in a restaurant, working shifts as a waitress. She moved in with her boyfriend and just after her 18th birthday became pregnant with her first child.

However, after having her second child she reassessed her options and decided that she would like to train to become a midwife.

Asher was told she would need GCSE English and Maths to be considered for the diploma, so she signed up for a free literacy course and passed with the equivalent of a GCSE B grade. She then progressed to a numeracy course. As a result Asher was able to apply for a three-year midwifery course, which she is due to finish this year.

technical skills, but they tend not to provide the sorts of skills that are needed in the modern workplace – such as the ability to communicate, team working, project management and time management," says Campbell. "And, even at some low skill levels, there are issues about attitudes to work and motivation."

Apprenticeships can address many of these issues and a recent review has seen the National Apprenticeship Service set up to engage employers and learners in the untapped and growing demand for Apprenticeships.

The government also hopes that its new 14 to 19 Diplomas will do much to address these basic problems. There will be 17 Diplomas in subjects ranging from hair and beauty studies, retail, construction and the built environment plus science. The aim is to roll out the Diplomas over the next three years, making them all available nationally by 2013. Ed Balls, secretary of state at the Department for Children, Schools and Families, hopes the Diplomas will close the gap between academic education and vocational training and that it will ultimately become the qualification of choice for young people.

Diplomas to develop broader skills

He believes the Diplomas will enable teenage students to develop the broader personal skills and attitudes that business and universities need. These include the ability to learn independently, think creatively, solve complex problems, manage time effectively, show determination and resilience, and work with others. He claims: "Diplomas will open up real opportunities for combining academic and practical options to allow every young person to make the most of their talents, whether they are progressing to further study, work or an Apprenticeship."

Ed Balls bases his confidence on the fact that employers have been at the centre of Diploma design to develop a qualification that explicitly addresses their needs: a curriculum built around real life work examples, high quality work experience, an emphasis on personal skills such as team-working and self-management as well as strong functional skills in English, maths and ICT.

The move has been welcomed by business. Richard Lambert, director general of the CBI, says: "The Diplomas are designed to ensure young people develop the skills they need – literacy, numeracy and employability – and make them realise how those skills are relevant to their working lives." But he warns: "Business must play its part by providing high-quality work experience that enables students to develop and apply the skills they've learnt in the classroom."

focus on large employers

The National Employer Service (NES) was set up in April 2002 by the Learning and Skills Council to provide a single point of contact for large national multi-site employers, who wish to hold a single contract with the Learning and Skills Council. It exists to help large companies and organisations make sense of Government skills strategy, the key players involved and to understand the support available for workforce development.

NES aim to be the catalyst for large employers to take ownership of, and invest in, the skills of their workforce. They provide independent, impartial advice and support and are currently working with more than 80 large firms, including Royal Mail, Sainsbury's, Tesco, British Aerospace, British Gas, Vodafone and McDonalds.

new UK Commission for Employment and Skills

The establishment of the UK Commission for Employment and Skills was a key recommendation of the independent report by Lord Sandy Leitch, Prosperity for all in the global economy – world-class skills (see page 10). The UKCES is chaired by Sir Michael Rake, chair of BT, and has the former director general of City & Guilds, Chris Humphries CBE, as its chief executive.

The UKCES provides vigorous and independent challenges, advising the government at the highest levels on employment and skills strategy, targets and policies and our progress towards the challenging competitiveness goals set by Lord Leitch. It has already been asked by the government to report on crucial issues, such as whether a statutory entitlement to training is appropriate and whether further institutional change is required to deliver better-integrated employment and skills services. There's never been a better time to improve skills.

where do I start?

Jessica Twentyman and Alison Coleman look at the steps companies can take to improve their skills base and unlock the potential of people

EXECUTIVE SUMMARY

☐ since its launch last year, almost 1,000 companies have made the government's Skills Pledge

☐ more than 30,000 organisations have now achieved the Investors in People training and development standard

☐ skills analyses can identify not only skills gaps but also hidden pools of talent in an organisation

☐ training and development plans must be 'holistic', covering every employee at every level

the Skills Pledge

What's the starting point for companies that want to take a fresh look at the skills their business should have – and discover the training staff need? One answer is to make the Skills Pledge.

Launched last summer, the Skills Pledge is a voluntary public commitment by the leadership of a company or organisation to support all its employees to develop their skills in the workplace and hence to be inspired to fulfil their potential.

Some companies who have made the Pledge already include Sainsbury, Superdrug, Interserve plc, Shell and BP. The spectrum of learning covers a vast area, which includes:

☐ achieving basic skills in literacy and numeracy

☐ Apprenticeships

☐ working towards relevant industry qualifications

MAKING THE SKILLS PLEDGE

VT Group, a defence and civil contractor, made the Skills Pledge in October 2007. "This isn't just a PR stunt," insisted Jo Robbins, group human resources director at the company. "We're signing up to some heavy duty work in the area of improving our skills base."

That's a complex task in a company as diverse as VT Group, she says, which has business interests ranging from shipbuilding to broadcast services.

Some areas of the business, she adds, have already benefited from major investments in learning and skills over recent years. "In our shipbuilding division, for example, we have an established learning and skills centre, which we run in partnership with union officials. That's enabled us to identify any problems with basic skills and [local] Eastleigh College has provided help where needed."

But in the company's education and skills division, ironically, the picture is less clear – so this is where VT Group will first work to identify gaps. "In this part of the business, there's a particularly large range of skills, from senior educational consultants who advise the governing boards of schools through to school caretakers, so the picture should be fascinating. "It will be interesting to shine a light into an area where the assumption might otherwise be that there are no skills gaps," says Robbins

- ☐ leadership and management training
- ☐ Foundation Degrees and other higher level qualifications

Jaine Clarke, director of Skills for Employers at the LSC, says that over 950 employers have made the Pledge. She says: "Not only [do] they want to show their commitment to their workforce, but also because it makes a difference to how their business performs."

The Skills Pledge is part of the government's drive to ensure that by 2020, the country is in the 'world's premier league for skills' – that it will be able to meet the recommendations of the Leitch review of skills (see chapter 1, page 10.)

Level 2 is the standard recommended in the Leitch Review of Skills. However, organisations are welcome to extend this commitment and help staff gain wider skills and additional qualifications, in line with their specific business needs. If they choose, employers can broaden the Skills Pledge to cover higher skills and qualifications. In other words, by signing up, they promise to help all employees achieve their full potential.

skills brokers

Skills Pledge employers will have access to the services of a skills broker, who can advise them on the most suitable training and qualifications for the business and its employees, and identify specific training programmes, such as foundation degrees, Diplomas and Apprenticeships. They can also ascertain what the funding costs will be and whether the business is eligible to draw on government funding. So what exactly will a skills broker do? What will happen when they come into your organisation?

Janet Powell is a Plymouth-based skills broker who works with companies throughout the south west, providing them with advice on their training needs, helping them to access funding and putting them in touch with training providers.

organisational needs analysis

A key part of her work, and a key reference point for her, is the Organisational Needs Analysis (ONA), a process that helps employers to analyse their business. It acts, Powell says, "as a prompt to start the dialogue rolling around current skills, where the company wants to go and the additional skills it will need to get there."

A lot of companies initially call a skills broker with a very specific need for training in areas such as first aid or manual handling. "But that's only the start of the conversation. Once we've had a chance to make them aware of the funding available for other kinds of training, they really start to consider the possibilities in a far more long-term way," says Powell.

The ONA is designed to capture information about skills, "from the shop floor to the boardroom", including the emotive subject of basic skills. "Because it's sensitive, companies tend to shy away from it. Often the issue doesn't really come up for discussion until a training provider has been called in to start an NVQ assessment and finds that the prospective candidate is lacking in basic skills – and that means that they'll need help with those, before they can even be considered for entry to an NVQ programme," she says.

Central to the success of training is the ability to find courses that match both employer and employee needs. Learning must be aligned with business objectives. With the help of a skills broker, organisations can be more confident they're making the right choices. The LSC's Jaine Clarke says: "The feedback we're getting from employers is that they like working with skills brokers. Through a broker, they are able to access the knowledge of somebody who is independent and impartial and looking after their interests." As well as identifying gaps, ONAs and skills analyses can help unearth previously hidden talents within the workforce. It's then a question of making sure there are training programmes in place to develop them.

impact of training on business performance

Ensuring that your employees have the right skills is crucial to the growth and success of your business. The business case for developing your staff is compelling – research shows that training can:

- increase productivity and quality of work

- increase profits

- reduce staff turnover and absenteeism

- improve customer satisfaction

- improve motivation

Training that achieves these results is typically:

- linked to business goals and performance

- part of a company-wide strategy

- focused on setting tangible objectives for employees

- part of a company policy, which sets out who is responsible for planning, implementing and evaluating training

A training needs analysis (TNA), carried out by a Train to Gain skills broker, is an effective way to identify any gaps between the skills your business needs and those your employees have. A TNA can help you clarify your objectives in training your staff, which is invaluable for ensuring that money is spent on training that will help your business to achieve its objectives.

A TNA will:

- ☐ analyse your business goals and the skills required to meet these goals
- ☐ determine whether you are changing your products or business processes and what information or training employees need to be effective in their job
- ☐ evaluate who you want to train and how best to reach them
- ☐ establish how employees will best accept and integrate training and their preferred learning method
- ☐ evaluate the training in place and decide what your company can and can't provide in the way of in-house training, funding and time
- ☐ assess which consultants or training providers can fill these gaps
- ☐ help you take a decision on which type of training fits your needs best

Investors in People

One, long-established route to ensuring a systematic, rigorous approach to employee development is the Investors in People (IiP) accreditation scheme. Employers may decide to apply for this standard alongside their commitment to the Skills Pledge. The scheme provides a flexible framework, which any organisation can adapt for its own requirements, to improve through its people.

Top five tips:

1. PLAN – to be successful an organisation and it's people need to know where it is going and how it aims to get there

2. COMMUNICATE – opening the channels of communication from top down and bottom up not only gives people the opportunity to contribute to the success of the business but also provides a mechanism to consult/inform everyone

3. LINK DEVELOPMENT TO BUSINESS NEEDS – by working with and helping people understand how their development will contribute to their success, that of the team and the organisation they will begin to understand how they contribute on a daily basis

4. LEAD BY EXAMPLE – top managers and managers leading in a

consistent and fair manner and being a role model for up and coming new supervisors/managers

5. PERFORMANCE REVIEWING – this can include the performance of the business against its targets, individual performance reviews (appraisals) through to staff perception surveys resulting in adjustments being made as necessary to meet customer, supplier or staff needs

Over the past 12 years independent research has consistently shown that the IiP Standard provides real business benefits to organisations of all sizes and across all sectors. Staff benefits include: increased morale, job satisfaction, better communication, plus more responsibility and involvement. There are many practical benefits of working towards and achieving the Standard, including:

- improved earnings, productivity and profitability – skilled and motivated people work harder and better, improving productivity

- customer satisfaction – Investors in People is central to helping employees become customer focused, enabling organisations to effectively meet customer needs

- improved motivation – motivation is improved through employees' greater involvement, personal development and recognition of their achievements. This leads to higher morale, improved retention rates, reduced absenteeism, readier acceptance of change and identification with the organisation's goals beyond confines of the job

- reduced costs and wastage – skilled and motivated people constantly examine their work to contribute towards reducing costs and wastage

- enhanced quality – Investing in people significantly improves the results of quality programmes

- competitive advantage through improved performance – Investor in People organisations develop a competitive edge

- public recognition

Currently, more than 30,000 UK organisations are recognised Investors in People, and the award is open to businesses of all types and sizes. It's possible to take a 'phased' approach to accreditation. Interserve, a services, maintenance and buildings group, has gained the IiP standard for three of its operating units, covering around one-fifth of the company's 25,000-strong workforce. It now aims to "roll out IiP recognition across the group". "It's simply common sense to give your workers a platform for achieving their own personal levels of potential, from basic skills to the highest levels of professional qualifications," says group head of human resources, Elaine Clarke.

The company's aim is to ensure that it offers equal skills and training opportunities enterprise-wide, in order to get the very most out of all of its employees.

pooling talent

Other companies are going to further lengths still, offering training to pools of talent currently outside their own organisations. London-based IT consultancy, ThoughtWorks, for example, is targeting female IT professionals who are already qualified but are on a 'career break' after raising families.

In a scheme sponsored by the not-for-profit organisation Equalitec, which promotes IT careers to women, the company is offering women the chance to update their skills with a four-week training course, where participants work on real-life IT projects alongside the company's own employees. "The IT industry moves very quickly, so it's easy for women who have taken a career break or maternity leave to feel that their skills are no longer relevant," explains John Galioto, managing director at ThoughtWorks. "But we aim to prove that this is not the case – and we have jobs on offer for those participants who impress us on this course," he says.

That kind of lateral thinking may become increasingly necessary in future. It's been estimated that around 70 per cent of the 2020 workforce is already of working age. So upskilling and reskilling the existing resource is going to be more vital than ever in the years to come.

Local Employment Partnerships offer a potential solution to this challenge – enhancing an employer's ability to draw on the untapped pools of talent while creating models upon which large and (increasingly) smaller employers can base their selection, induction and training processes. Resources have already been funnelled into LEPs with the work done to create Sector Employability Toolkits for 9 skills sectors working with the LSC and Jobcentre Plus.

training and the small business

> **Greater flexibility and availability of training services means more and more companies are realising the value of investing in training. Laura Mazur and Alison Coleman report**

"How do I get the skills and expertise for diversification, business development and growth?" "How can I make sure my staff feel that they're valued and that their potential will be realised?" "What will happen to the company when key people leave? How can I identify and prepare the next generation of managers and directors?"

These are common questions in business. But for directors of small and medium-sized companies they can be particularly challenging. The obvious answer 'invest in more training and development' can seem unrealistic to companies struggling with limited budgets and resources. However training and development needn't be costly.

Yet the questions won't go away. And they need to be asked. This chapter looks at various learning and skills solutions for smaller companies. It's divided into three parts, each focusing on a particular small-business need.

EXECUTIVE SUMMARY

- ☐ companies that close the skills gap see demonstrable benefits and financial returns

- ☐ business leaders are joining forces with management schools to share their expertise with entrepreneurs

- ☐ Investors in People and Train to Gain offer valuable lessons for SMEs

- ☐ in-house mentoring can be a cost-effective solution to employee training and development

part one: skills for growth

Growth is built on identifying opportunities, understanding what skills are needed to take advantage of them, and finding the people who have those skills – whether they're inside or outside the organisation.

It's all very simple in theory; but for hard-pressed owner-managers, it can be very difficult in practice. Thankfully, there are more places for entrepreneurs to turn.

The government's Train to Gain service, run by the LSC (see chapter 2, page 16) offers free, impartial skills analysis about what you need now and what you might need for the future. The LSC estimated last year that 80 per cent of those using the service were new to training and came mainly from small businesses.

Local Employment Partnerships do not directly involve post-recruitment activities but address retention by encouraging effective selection and preparation of candidates in the first place. LEPs enable employers to choose from a range of measures whilst helping new staff fit into their company. When pre-employment training is involved Train to Gain is a natural development as people are already tuned in to a programme of learning.

The benefits of Train to Gain for small businesses are three-fold: a single point of contact, saved time and access to government funding. Train to Gain addresses the age-old concern often voiced by small businesses of not understanding the training and government arena and being redirected to different places to access support.

The skills broker is the single point of contact and will source provision on behalf of the employer, according to your needs, whether you want a single provider to meet all your needs or you prefer to work with a range of specialist providers. Once the needs are identified, the skills broker will advise you on which aspects of the training are subject to government subsidy.

As part of Train to Gain's expansion, funding for small business owners or managers who wish to undertake training to improve their leadership or

POWERCHEX: STEPS BEFORE EXPANSION

Alexandra Kelly set up her business, Powerchex, in 2005. Now 27-strong, London-based Powerchex specialises in pre-employment screening and employment reference solutions for financial services firms.

Kelly spotted the gap for the vetting service while doing risk management in the City and analysing human resources processes. Despite being turned down by the Dragon's Den investors, the business, she says, is now well on course to reaching a turnover of a million.

She has been a keen advocate of the Shell Step placement scheme from the beginning. In fact, within three months of opening her doors she had the first student in. "The great thing is that the Shell Steps website is very interactive. You describe your project and they match you to students and send CVs."

In summer 2007, she decided to take two students to work on two different projects. One was asked to look at the company's processes and see where they could be streamlined and possibly automated. The other, Toby Smith, a history student from York University, was asked to help design and implement a PR programme for the company in its bid to get its name better known.

Smith spent his first four weeks doing research that he could then publicise. The research looked at the extent to which job applications for banks and other financial institutions were 'embellished'. The results showed that a more stringent vetting regime in the City had cut down on dishonesty – although there was a rise in failure to disclose criminal records.

Armed with these findings, Smith hit the phones, repeatedly cold-calling more than 100 journalists. His hard work paid off: the research attracted a wide range of coverage, including a piece in the Guardian.

Links to the company website from search engines rose by over 3,000 hits, while Kelly calculates that savings in promotional and consultancy costs were well over £16,000 and £2,500 respectively.

Did the company pick up any new customers from the PR blitz? "I don't think so, but we did get a lot of awareness," says Kelly. She believes it is no coincidence that the company was named Service Business of the Year at the national NatWest Start-up Awards in November 2007.

management skills is increasing from £4m to £30m.

Derbyshire based architecture firm Bi Design has significantly benefited from the Train to Gain service. Architect Darryn Buttrill, 39, launched Bi Design Architecture in 1998. In order to develop his business further, expand and provide more support for his staff, he contacted Train to Gain. Skills broker Geraldine Wilson helped source relevant courses and training.

Darryn enrolled on a mentoring programme, which involved 15 half-day mentoring scheme sessions, with a business professional who he can talk to about any issues he has, such as redundancies, staff recruitment and general business management.

Meanwhile, another employee completed an NVQ in Business Administration. All of this came at the cost of only £250 and since training, Bi Design's profits have been increased by 50 per cent.

Darryn said: "Thanks to help from Geraldine and my mentor I now feel far more confident in how I run my business. Having someone to talk through any problems or queries makes all the difference, as you don't feel so isolated.

"Because of this, operationally the business is better managed, and the investment I have made in staff training and development has really paid off with higher retention and greater output. We have such a great team here and I really look forward to taking the business even further in the future."

An alternative solution is to hire new staff temporarily to boost headcount while you work out your longer term needs. The Shell Step placement scheme, created by Shell UK, offers SMEs the chance to plug skills gaps through undergraduate staff. University students in their second or penultimate year of study come into a company to work on a project for eight weeks.

The scheme, which has been running since 1986, makes sure that the placement is a good fit. The company gets a valuable and cost-effective pair of hands. Andrew Eddy, director of Shell UK, explains the benefits: "For the businesses that take part, the value of these work placements is two-fold. They can fulfil their commercial needs in the short-term: for example, Step students have helped to produce new and enhanced products, marketing strategies, bespoke software, efficient administration processes and lots more.

"Perhaps even more importantly, temporary work placements can help businesses identify where their skills gaps lie and enable them to address these over the longer term."

Young and growing companies need expert advice as well as manpower, however. And there's an increasing number of networks and 'academies'

THE WINNING BUSINESS ACADEMY

The Winning Business Academy is the first sales academy dedicated to helping budding entrepreneurs in the north west benefit from the skills and experience of people from larger companies. It was set up in February 2007 by consultant John Leach in conjunction with the University of Manchester Incubator Company (UMIC).

By the end of the year it had seen almost 300 companies go through the programme. It is sponsored by the Anglo-Irish Bank, The Royal Bank of Scotland, the Manchester Investment Agency (MIDAS) and Baker Tilly.

UMIC'S Tony Walker emphasises that the approach the Academy takes is grounded in commercial basics: "The Academy teaches set-piece methodologies for high-performance growth. It's based on observational research showing what the best in breed in the FTSE 100 and FTSE 250 do. Small companies often lose sight of the strategic direction in the day-to-day activities; we re-focus and re-energise them."

One successful graduate is Mobysoft, a young Manchester-based technology company set up in 2003 by Derek Steele. He had an idea for using automated SMS text messaging as a cost-effective way for different organisations such as housing associations to communicate with people.

By May 2006, he had a nucleus of clients in the housing sector and moved into office space at UMIC. He decided to take advantage of the new Academy venture: "We had ambitions for fast growth and knew we needed to be a lot more sales-focused." As a result of its work with the Academy, the company has now set up a documented sales process.

Leach believes the Academy could be a template for other initiatives: "It is essentially a business format that binds together the aspirations of entrepreneurs within the Greater Manchester region, but we will then be spinning it out into other parts of the UK."

designed to make sure they get just that. Some specialise in key areas of commercial development.

The Winning Business Academy, for example, aims to help young businesses understand the importance of strategic selling (see above). It was set up by John Leach, chief executive of the business and coaching consultancy Winning Pitch, and Tony Walker, business incubator manager at the University of Manchester Incubator Company (UMIC).

Says Leach: "Entrepreneurs can have great ideas but can be ineffective in taking that proposition and generating commercial revenue streams from them". His academy aims to fill the gap.

HAPPY: STANDARD BEARER FOR PEOPLE MANAGEMENT

Happy is a London-based company offering training in areas such as IT, leadership, management, customer service and emotional intelligence. Its founder, Henry Stewart, set the company up 20 years ago based on his belief that a business benefits if employees feel good about working there.

When managing director Cathy Busani joined 13 years ago, the company had 10 people and did only IT training. Now with 50 staff, it tailors training to client needs. It has earned a raft of awards for customer service, workplace culture and corporate social responsibility.

Busani says the company decided to embrace the IiP standard in 1997 so that it could get external feedback on what it was doing well and what needed to change. "We wanted to check that we were on the right track and not just applauding ourselves," explains Busani. "Getting an external body like IiP, which is so well-respected, to say you are getting it right is fantastic."

IiP also highlighted areas for improvement, she says: "Ten years ago, our inductions weren't as structured as they should be and had left some new people feeling it was a bit hit and miss. So we were able to adapt and change." Happy achieved its third IiP accreditation in 2006 (under the scheme, companies have to reapply every three years).

Busani has no doubts about the business case for IiP: "The easiest way to measure it is the very low staff turnover," she says. "If we have a staff vacancy, we have 200 people on our job list waiting to hear from us. We save a lot of money on recruitment because people tend not to leave."

getting closer to clients

Other academies offer professional business advisers the chance to hone their skills – and, by extension, those of their clients. The Coutts & Co private Banking Academy, for example, was set up as a joint initiative with the Cranfield School of Management's Bettany Centre for Entrepreneurial Performance and Economics last year. During 2007-8 more than 100 bankers from Coutts private bank will take part in a series of programmes focused on entrepreneurship.

As Nick Gornall, Coutts head of private banking, entrepreneurs and southern region, explains: "Coutts are established as the private bank of choice for successful entrepreneurs. These sorts of people also go through the Cranfield business growth programme. The joint initiative with Cranfield will ensure the advice we provide to small business clients remains relevant, informed and market leading."

part two: staff retention

Retaining key staff is of growing concern to companies of all sizes, but for smaller companies, it can mean the difference between survival or not. If a talented sales person walks, for example, a good chunk of the business can leave with them.

But there's a conundrum: even though training is a proven route to retention, small companies often shy away from the idea either because they see it as something only big companies do or because they fear the newly-trained person will just go and find a better job.

PERMADOOR: RECRUITS AND RETAINS STAFF

Permadoor, part of the Epwin Group and with factories in Malvern and Upton upon Severn, make composite doors and are the UK's leading supplier to the social housing sector.

The company is reaping benefits from its rolling programme of NVQ training delivered by the Learning and Skills Council through the government's Train to Gain service. Permadoor has been working with Telford College of Arts and Technology to deliver its NVQ Level 2 in Performing Manufacturing Operations or Technical Service. So far, nearly 60 of the company's 71 production employees have undertaken training.

Rob Millar, Permadoor's Manufacturing Manager says: "We set it up as a way of getting new people into the company because we offer an NVQ qualification when we employ people and we're looking to retain people once they are trained. They get an additional pay allowance once they get their NVQ. At Upton particularly there is not a big pool of people to employ, whereas the Malvern factory is on an industrial estate.

"There is competition to employ good people, so we have to offer something that other employers do not. I feel it works well for both parties, the employer and the employee, so we both gain something – I get loyal well trained staff who understand the business, they get a formal qualification. This is a great incentive to encourage and retain staff – some people have moved on in their job role to train for a second qualification, so the process goes on."

---

faulty reasoning

This is understandable but faulty reasoning, argues June Williams, director of quality and delivery partners at Investors in People (IiP). "This problem of

SNOWDROP: HELPING PEOPLE FULFILL THEIR POTENTIAL

Snowdrop, a provider of HR and payroll software services, employs around 150 people on sites in Witney, Oxfordshire and in Glasgow.

The company operates an internal mentoring system that plays a key role in staff training and development, and with a policy of promoting from within, has also proved valuable in identifying potential management talent.

Client services team manager Mandy Keegan, who is based in the Glasgow office, joined the company six years ago as a trainee software developer, a role that she soon began to feel was too technical and 'not quite right for her'.

She explains: "Although the company was much smaller at that time, with around 50 employees, there was a strong mentoring culture and as a direct result of that my manager, who had been mentoring me, quickly recognised the fact that my skills and capabilities would be of greater value to the company in the project management department. I transferred there and immediately felt much happier in that role."

Eighteen months ago she was promoted to a management position in the same department. "Mentoring really does give you an opportunity to identify people's real strengths and weaknesses and give them an opportunity to fulfil their true potential," she adds.

"Without that mentoring support and the chance to work in a role where I felt I could really shine, I would almost certainly have left the company quite early on. Instead I am enjoying a thoroughly rewarding career, and as a mentor myself, I like to think that I have helped to provide others with similar opportunities."

training key people who then leave comes up time and again" she says. "And, of course, people might leave. But you will get so much more out of someone while they are there if you train them properly. Also, when companies talk about key people, they should remember that the whole company is your talent. If you are not getting the best out of them what's the point?"

As the story of Happy shows (see page 36), the IiP standard can be applied successfully to companies of all sizes. And, says Williams, small businesses are among those who benefit most from it: it makes them think more carefully about how to find and keep the skills they need and also about their overall business goals.

It is crucial to assess skills gaps at all levels of the business, including senior management (see information on TNA, page 27). Include yourself in this if you are an owner-manager. You may need to develop your entrepreneurial and technical skills as the business grows.

PETERSEN STAINLESS STEEL RIGGING: EMPLOYEE DEVELOPMENT

Petersen Stainless Rigging, based at Blaydon, Gateshead, is a specialist manufacturer of stainless steel and rigging products for the marine and architectural industries.

With a growing commitment to workforce development, Petersen needed to identify which basic skills its staff lacked, and address people's needs. Through the Train to Gain service, the company was able to analyse which training would be most beneficial to the staff, and set up the necessary programme through the Sunderland Engineering Training Association.

Sixteen employees, almost half the workforce, pursued NVQ Level 2 qualifications in engineering production, with the resulting improvement in workforce skills boosting productivity and helping to secure future growth.

Company secretary Gary Wales says: "As a small company, there are a lot of things that we do – such as mentoring – on an informal basis. Once we had this platform of basic Level 2 skills, we found that people felt more confident and that their expectations and aspirations were higher.

"That has made it much easier for the management team to spot individual skills and identify those with real flair and potential. Training has definitely helped us to plan for the future."

part three: succession planning

Spotting potential successors in a small company can be just as challenging as identifying future managers from low levels of staff in large organisations. It takes a management team that is properly skilled in observation and communication, a well structured and focused training strategy, and an open company culture. Apprenticeships play a key role in succession planning (see case study on page 70).

benefits of mentoring

One technique used by many companies is mentoring, where experienced senior members of staff work closely with newer or more junior employees to monitor progress and encourage two-way feedback. It can bring several benefits:

- ☐ skills gaps can be identified more easily, allowing training to be better targeted towards the needs of individual staff and the business

- ☐ there is greater opportunity for management to identify progress and spot the rising stars who will take the organisation forward

- ☐ members of the senior team can pass on their knowledge and expertise to newer recruits in a more informal way and engender a company-wide understanding of the company culture.

Despite this, and the fact that mentoring is virtually cost free, many companies have no scheme in place.

Ian Young, managing director of Training and Development Resource (TDR), a Gateshead-based Train to Gain skills broker, says: "Informal mentoring, where you take someone under your wing to guide and develop them used to be prevalent in companies, particularly in heavy industry, a few years ago.

"Sadly, much of that type of staff development was lost during the post recession era, when the staff training budget was among the first things to be cut," he adds.

He agrees that mentoring can be useful as a way of spotting talent within the workplace, but thinks it shouldn't be seen as an instant solution to succession planning. "In some ways, mentoring is an extension of the induction process. It only really becomes useful for talent spotting later, when the person you are mentoring has become fully engaged with the company and started to feel valued."

Mentors are usually selected on the basis of their experience and their position in the business. They should also be excellent communicators, able to talk, listen, offer career development advice, teach new techniques, and introduce the people they are mentoring to new challenges and experiences.

tomorrow's workforce

British manufacturers are working with skills councils to expand Apprenticeships. Laura Mazur looks at the benefits

Motivating junior staff, particularly those with few qualifications and skills, can be tricky. They often have neither the training nor the interest to stay the course. The Diploma will help improve the preparation of young people for the world of work through its innovative curriculum. But, once in work, it is becoming increasingly essential to equip those junior employees with the tools they need to help companies survive in the face of an ageing workforce and global competition.

Apprenticeships are so important to our future success that we're doubling the number, and the resurgence of interest in training schemes for young people is contributing to the government's target of 500,000 new Apprenticeship places by 2020. It also explains the growing number of productive partnerships between companies, the various Sector Skills Council (SSCs) and the Further Education sector.

The government has asked the LSC to set up the National Apprenticeship Service to have end-to-end accountability for the Apprenticeship programme.

EXECUTIVE SUMMARY

☐ combining an in-house scheme with an NVQ can create a powerful motivational tool

☐ retired and older employees can help pass skills and knowledge on to the new generation

☐ Apprenticeships help fulfil a company's obligations – to both shareholders and stakeholders

☐ engaging in Diploma delivery helps school leavers prepare for the world of work

☐ training and development is a proven staff retention tool

MULBERRY: A STITCH IN TIME

Mulberry is a luxury leather goods and clothes company whose products are highly-prized in the fashion world.

Its reputation is built on quality and craftsmanship; in other words, on skills. So when the pool of local skills started to dry up, the company knew it had to take action. A succession plan for Mulberry's highly successful handbag factory in Somerset exposed potentially serious problems. "It showed we had an ageing but highly skilled workforce – which is fantastic in terms of loyalty – but it meant that if we didn't start to bring in new young skills over a period of time we might not have a workforce at all," says Ian Scott, supply director.

The factory, which produces 30 per cent of the luxury handbags, is a lynchpin of Mulberry. But without skills, its future was under threat. Scott hit upon the idea of re-introducing Apprenticeships. However, while there was an Apprenticeship programme for footwear manufacture, the Apprenticeship for leather goods had disappeared. So he had a choice: create a stand-alone Mulberry Apprenticeship or do it officially through National Vocational Qualifications (NVQs) and City and Guilds. He opted for the latter, believing that offering employees the chance to gain a nationally recognised qualification would increase staff morale and motivation – and put something back into the local community and his business.

His first step was to discuss his ideas with relevant people in organisations such as Business Link, the LSC's Train to Gain and Skillfast-UK. The problem was that the only college of further education that had a lot of skills in leather goods was in Northampton, and Mulberry wanted to train its apprentices on site.

The solution was a relationship, brokered through Skillfast-UK, between Mulberry and nearby Bridgwater College. Bridgwater would oversee the NVQ side of the qualifications and assessments, and any training in English, maths and communication, but sub-contract the technical areas to retired individuals skilled in making leather goods. The programme began with nine apprentices in August 2006. The plan is to take on a new group each year, training them in skills such as stitching and cutting and, if need be, in English and maths.

By the end of last year, six were left. Says Scott: "We think that is pretty good – and maybe higher than we would have anticipated, particularly since the first group were trailblazers. Those six are really motivated and enjoying it. It has also given a message to all the staff that we are here for the long term."

People 1st is the SSC for the hospitality, leisure, travel and tourism industries. Currently worth more than £135bn a year, the sector stands to make huge profits from the London 2012 Olympics – provided it can recruit and retain the right people. Staff 'churn' rates in the sector are notoriously high. People 1st's chief executive officer, Brian Wisdom, emphasises the benefits of training: "By providing your staff with the right training, you demonstrate a commitment to developing them, which in turn can improve their motivation and company loyalty. It can actually help to reduce staff turnover, so it doesn't make sense for businesses to use that as an excuse not to train."

Linda Florance, chief executive Skillfast-UK, the SSC that oversees the apparel, footwear and textiles sector, notes that companies in her sector are finally beginning to get their act together in terms of training younger employees: "For quite a long time, we went through stagnation in improving skills. But that's changing now as employers recognise there isn't a flood of people from big companies they can recruit from. They actually need to do it themselves." Which is what enterprising companies such as Mulberry and Sheffield Forgemasters are doing.

Simon Witts, director of Safety, Quality & Training at Flybe, one of the first employers to receive accreditation of their own training adds: "By becoming an

SHEFFIELD FORGEMASTERS: ENGINEERING A CHANGE

Sheffield Forgemasters is the world's largest independently owned forgemaster, producing high-quality engineered products to a wide range of industries, including defence, oil and gas and power generation. It is also playing a leading role in improving crucial engineering skills for the industry as a whole through its highly praised Apprenticeship programme.

The company, which is 200 years old, was rescued from closure through a management buyout in 2005, led by chief executive Dr Graham Honeyman, who had been working with the company since 2001.

An analysis of the workforce showed that many of the employees were approaching retirement, making a succession planning strategy vital. According to Semta, the skills council for science, engineering and manufacturing technologies, the problems Forgemasters faced are far from unusual. "Skills shortages in the engineering sector is a big issue," says Ian Carnell, the council's head of learning strategies.

Realising it had to act before the skills of older, experienced workers were lost, the company worked with Semta and its subsidiary MetSkill, the strategic skills body for the UK metals industry, to design an ambitious Apprenticeship programme.

The company is currently training 61 apprentices from a total of 708 employees for careers across all departments. Semta and Metskill have helped ensure that the training is tailored exactly to the company's needs. Apprentices can work towards qualifications such as NVQs that will develop their job skills. They can also go on to learn more specialised skills through

SHEFFIELD FORGEMASTERS: ENGINEERING A CHANGE

the BTEC and City and Guilds qualifications, combined with a work-based key-skills learning programme to develop numerical, IT and science skills linked directly to their jobs.

In addition to learning new skills through specific training modules, the Forgemasters apprentices will learn from individually appointed mentors at the plant, many of whom have more than 30 years of industry experience and knowledge to pass on.

"There are highly skilled and motivated young people out there who need to be given an opportunity to shine, says Honeyman. "This is a unique company in the things we make and how we make them. We have an ageing workforce that must be replaced. We have to train our own workforce."

Investing heavily in Apprenticeships to prepare the company for future growth and increased productivity in the face of fierce competition from the Far East and the pound's strength is paying off. "In the last four years, sales have more than doubled from our River Don site," Honeyman adds.

accredited training provider we will have the ability to deliver officially recognised courses specifically designed to cater for our staff and business needs, increasing our competitiveness and recognising the hard work of our employees."

sectors in the spotlight

The construction, engineering and IT industries face acute skills shortages. But, find Jessica Twentyman and Alison Coleman, much is being done to address the problem

construction

Despite an influx of workers from the newer EU countries, the UK construction industry faces a major skills challenge.

Over the next five years, Britain is expected to experience a building bonanza, placing a strain on the availability of skilled labour, according to industry forecasts.

Construction output, already on a high, is predicted to grow by almost 11 per cent by 2011, led by a surge in schools construction, increased spending on transport and projects for the London Olympics, according to ConstructionSkills, the skills council for the sector. That means that employment in the industry will need to rise by almost a sixth to 2.8 million by 2011, compared with 2.4 million in 2005. Put another way, the industry needs 87,000 new recruits a year to meet demand.

EXECUTIVE SUMMARY

- the building industry needs around a quarter of a million new recruits by 2011

- around half of the UK's engineering companies are experiencing recruitment difficulties

- the number of applicants for maths and computer science degrees has declined

- collaboration with government bodies and FE institutes is providing effective solutions

BE ONSITE: RE-SKILLING THE LOCAL LABOUR FORCE

Construction giant Bovis Lend Lease UK, through its Local Employment Partnership with Jobcentre Plus, has launched a new, not-for-profit training organisation, Be Onsite, aimed at addressing skills shortages, in partnership with the London Development Agency and the Learning and Skills Council (LSC).

A key objective for Be Onsite is to map the skills that are needed and identify how they can be provided through specialist accredited training providers. The organisation will also provide a co-ordinated, single point of contact through which employers can access the local labour market.

"The idea of Be Onsite is modelled on the job shops we have been operating on most of our major construction sites over the past 12 years. This linkage of local people to construction training and jobs has resulted in almost 10,000 people finding construction employment, and a further 11,000 people going into retail jobs," says Murray Coleman, chief executive of Bovis Lend Lease UK.

"It's a great concept: it helps long-term unemployed people overcome barriers to employment; the local community benefits, because skilled tradespeople remain in the local area long after the construction project has finished; and the construction industry can fill some of the many vacancies attributed to the current skills shortage."

Encouraging more companies to invest in training for new and existing staff is seen as vital to improving the industry's performance and ensuring the provision of high-quality construction services.

In 2006, around 4,100 construction employers invested in the longer-term development of their workforce by adopting a training and development plan. But with so many new recruits needed this needs to become universal.

industry-wide benefits

Mike Bialyj, director of advisory services at ConstructionSkills, says: "Training is the best way for construction employers to develop their business, and by investing in their employees they also contribute to the industry as a whole."

ConstructionSkills provides skills training and support for employers, anticipating the needs of the industry and responding with a range of appropriate measures. Initiatives include a new Apprenticeship programme, onsite training and

LSC AND THE OLYMPICS CHALLENGE

The Learning and Skills Council (LSC) has pledged to expand the range and quality of work-based learning across London to meet the challenges the capital faces in hosting the London 2012 Olympic and Paralympic Games.

Harvey Redgrave is the LSC's Director of Economic Development for the Olympics. He says: "Our aim is to use the Olympics and Paralympics as an opportunity to raise skills levels and aspirations across London."

Given the demands the 2012 games will place on the building industry, the LSC is determined to increase the number of trained construction workers in London and is working with ConstructionSkills to make the Olympics site a National Skills Academy for Construction.

One part of this is the Plant Skills Training Centre at Eton Manor. This is delivering practical training on equipment such as dumpers, telescopic handlers and excavators. The National Skills Academy for Construction will coordinate training for people to get the skills they need to win work on the Olympic park. By the end of the programme, at least 2,000 people will be on trainee Apprenticeships or work placements at the Olympic Park.

Curdy had been working as a plasterer when a friend who worked in construction said he might be able to help get him a job labouring on the Olympic Park site. Curdy got a place on the four-day Slinger Signaller (Banksman) course at the Plant Training Centre. Curdy said: "I hope that I can move forward from labouring and start to work as a Banksman soon."

As a former 200m and 400m track champion at his high school in Jamaica, Curdy will be keeping a keen eye on the sporting action when the Games arrive in 2012. "It would be good to keep working on something as big as the London 2012 Olympic and Paralympic Games, right near my home."

assessments for experienced workers, university scholarships and a national skills academy for construction, which champions employer-led training.

ConstructionSkills grants are available to support employer programmes aimed at qualifying existing workers, improving health and safety standards, and training new recruits.

grants for non-core skills training

As well as securing funding for construction-based training programmes, construction companies that have a formal training and development plan can also claim grants for training in other areas that benefit their business, including computer skills, accountancy and administration.

Diploma in Construction and the Built Environment

The new Diploma will be taught from September 2008. Combining practical skills development with theoretical and technical knowledge, it will give young people a better insight into what the sector is like to work in

engineering

A recent survey of 500 companies from the Institution of Engineering and Technology (IET) shows that, when it comes to skills, confidence among companies in the sector is low.

The number of respondents who expected to face difficulties in recruiting adequate suitably qualified engineers, technicians or technologists over the next four years had risen to over half (52 per cent) in 2007, from 40 per cent the previous year. With teaching beginning this year, the Diploma in Engineering, developed with employers to meet their requirements, will soon provide a new route into the profession.

recruiting from overseas

To meet current needs, many British companies are turning to countries such as India, China and South Africa to plug the skills gaps, says Robin McGill, the IET's chief executive, with 48 per cent of companies recruiting from overseas in the past 12 months to cover specific skills shortages.

"The engineering and technology sector is vital to the future prosperity of the UK's economy, and skills shortages put the future growth, success and competitive advantage of many businesses into serious doubt. The UK desperately needs to increase the pool of engineers and technicians to meet demand," he says.

Bob Taylor, a member of the executive board of E.ON, the UK's largest integrated power company, agrees: "As a sector, we're facing particular challenges

E.ON: EMPOWERING THE WORKFORCE

Power company E.ON is taking a 'holistic' approach to the skills problem, trying to ensure there are training and development opportunities for all.

Last year, it announced the creation of the E.ON Engineering Academy, an 'umbrella' organisation that brings together a wide range of internal initiatives with 'bespoke' NVQs and foundation degrees offered by Walsall College and Aston University. It is designed for all levels of the technical workforce, from craftsmen to professional engineers. E.ON hopes to map out a career path that will see people progress all the way from Level 1 NVQ to full honours degrees and chartered engineer status.

At the same time, it's "scouting for talent" outside the existing workforce. In November, the company announced that 12 budding young engineers from schools in Walsall and Chesterfield would be taking part in its first-ever Young Apprenticeship Programme. For the final two years of the students' GCSE courses, they will each spend a total of 50 days at E.ON, working with professional engineers to gain practical experience.

Students who show real potential could also ultimately progress to E.ON's Advanced Apprenticeship Programme, which will help to fast-track them to an engineering career with the company. At the other end of the scale, in 2006 E.ON continued collaboration with the Warwick Business School to deliver its Challenge of Leadership programme to around 200 of its senior managers.

brought on by a period of sustained reinvestment in our assets and infrastructure – and we know we need to match that with investment in the skills we'll need to run them," he says.

"However, we can't continue 'living on the legacy' of the layoffs of the 1990s that kept us with a stocked pool of skills for some time."

Industry bodies such as the IET have much work to do in helping member organisations to address these challenges. "It's incumbent on the whole industry to put aside competitive pressures and work together to share best practice in skills, education and training," says Taylor. .

information technology

The skills shortage in the IT sector is well-publicised by the vast numbers of companies that have outsourced IT processes to third-party providers, mainly

EDS: CONNECTING UP TO THE FUTURE

The IT services company EDS, which currently employs 16,000 people in the UK, has taken significant steps to ensure that the steady stream of job applicants to its door doesn't dry up. Its initiatives include working with schools, collaborating with companies such as Microsoft and Cisco in the design of an industry-led IT diploma, and Apprenticeships, from which around 600 young people have graduated in the past 10 years.

"As EDS suffers natural workforce attrition, the talent pool of replacements is likely to reduce, and we believe it is our responsibility to be significantly involved in efforts to enhance the current and existing talent pool in critical skills areas," says Alastair Mann, EDS's head of global workforce management for Europe, the Middle East and Africa.

It's not just about attracting new skills; it's also about developing the ones the company has in-house. "We have a strong culture of allowing employees to 'own' their careers and giving them every support they need to do that," Mann continues. "So our corporate learning catalogue has details of over 7,000 classes, covering specific technology areas, business fundamentals in presentation and communication, and other areas such as project management and sales."

Some employees will take these courses just because they're interested, he says. Others will be required to take them by their line manager, as part of the performance review processes.

Having recently made the Skills Pledge, EDS is now turning its hand to ensuring that skills up to Level 2 are covered as well. "That's never been a benchmark internally for us before, so it will be interesting to see if we have any gaps there that we didn't know about. It will take us deeper into areas of the business, such as consultancy support roles, to identify groups that need more support," Mann adds.

in India, in recent years. Price is a big factor here, of course, but availability of skills, in areas such as software development, is also a major draw.

According to a study conducted by IT systems integrator and consultancy Capgemini, Europe outsources two per cent of its IT operations, a figure that rises to eight per cent in the UK.

The student intake for maths and computer sciences in the UK has dropped by a quarter since 2002, according to the National Audit Office. What's more, one in 10 maths and computer sciences undergraduates drop out after just one year.

As the case study on EDS shows, solving the problem depends on collaboration. Businesses need to work with each other to improve the outlook for their sector and, crucially, they need to work with the LSC and schools and colleges.

The new Diploma in Information Technology, developed and supported by sector leaders such as Cisco, IBM, Microsoft, Logica, Oracle and Vodafone provides a key opportunity for employers to engage with local educational partners to help ensure young people receive an education that speaks directly to industry needs, increasing the supply of appropriately qualified and motivated new entrants to the workforce.

Sector Employment Toolkits

Employer commitment to Local Employment Partnerships comes from a wide range of sectors. Sector Employability Toolkits for nine of these have been agreed with the LSC and Jobcentre Plus. The SET for the retail sector, developed with Skillsmart Retail Ltd (the Sector Skills Council for retail) features:

- an **employability checklist** to identify the attitude, skills and behaviour expected at the point of entry

- a **recruitment checklist** specifying the minimum entry requirements such as literacy, numeracy and manual dexterity

- a **selection process** to support interviews, open days and assessments

- a Routeway programme consisting of **2 week's training** equipping individuals with the skills required to enter employment or benefit from up to 3 weeks **work trial**

Our
future.
**It's in
our hands.**

Leadership,
management,
collaboration...
it's these **skills** that really
start to make **numbers**
move for your
business.

You've employed the best people available for your business, but it's the skills you don't necessarily find on paper that can really help your company flourish. People skills like leadership and management allow the financial sector to really excel, but they can often be overlooked. Train to Gain offers the impartial advice and support your company needs to ensure your staff won't just have a head for figures; they'll have all the relevant skills to make those figures work even harder.

For more information visit
traintogain.gov.uk or call on 0800 015 55 45.

Train to
Gain

training for innovation

Partnerships with the LSC, Skills Councils and universities, colleges and training organisations are helping to prepare business for tomorrow's world. Alison Coleman reports

Innovation is at the heart of business success: if organisations cannot innovate, their long-term future is in doubt.

In the global marketplace, the ability to come up with new ideas and exploit new opportunities is essential for businesses of all sizes. It depends on high-level skills in the workforce. In other words: high-quality training is, quite literally, vital for business.

building partnerships with higher education

EXECUTIVE SUMMARY

☐ the ability to innovate and adapt, so vital for the modern business, depends on high-level skills

☐ foundation degrees are plugging the gap in the market for employer and employee-friendly training

☐ the Train to Gain service directs employers towards the courses that deliver tangible returns

☐ placement schemes are giving smaller businesses access to top-level student talent

One way that organisations can foster a stronger culture of innovation is by forming partnerships with higher education institutions to develop and deliver high-quality study programmes, including diplomas and degrees, tailored specifically to their needs. Launched three years ago, foundation degrees are vocationally focused qualifications designed in partnership with employers to provide organisations of all sizes, from across all sectors, with the skills to 'future proof' their businesses.

EMPLOYER-LED TRAINING

A foundation degree in utilities management has been developed in response to the requirements of United Utilities, which serves nearly three million customers in the north west of England.

The company had identified a need for a higher level training programme to develop specialist technical knowledge alongside more general leadership and management skills.

United Utilities, Foundation Degree Forward and the skills council Energy and Utility Skills worked with the University of Central Lancashire and Bolton Community College to develop a pilot programme.

The programme needed to be industry-specific and 'modular' to enable employees to study in 'blocks' and complete the course within two financial years. The first cohort enrolled in March 2006; and a second group two months later. There are currently 22 students on the pilot.

Professor Derek Longhurst, chief executive of Foundation Degree Forward, the national body that supports the development of foundation degrees, says: "These courses provide opportunities for work-based learning and the accreditation of existing employer training, and can be designed around workforce commitments. There is an emphasis in such programmes on the application of knowledge and skills in the workplace: foundation degrees support greater productivity and employee motivation.

"Many companies have found that the development of a foundation degree programme for employees can raise performance and retain the best staff."

keeping competitive in the global market

Other initiatives launched through partnerships between businesses and the higher education world are also helping to deliver and maintain the skills needed to keep key UK industries ahead in the global market.

Information Technology Management for Business (ITMB) is a new IT honours degree course. Designed by some of the IT industry's biggest employers, in conjunction with e-skills, the skills council for IT and telecoms, the ITMB equips graduates with the tools they need to lead the industry.

Karen Price, CEO of e-skills UK, says: "Attracting new talent into the IT and telecoms workforce is vital for the UK's global competitiveness. Employers of IT professionals often recruit from non-IT disciplines to obtain skills that are now essential for the IT workforce. IT-related degrees that aim to prepare students for modern careers in IT must adapt to reflect the broader range of capabilities required to be successful. The success of the ITMB degrees shows how urgently such innovative courses are needed."

learning through work

Employers have a key role in investing in individuals to bring out the best in them which is why many of them play an active part in employee training and development. The new scheme to accredit in-house training means employers can win recognition for their qualifications and/or gain approval to

LOTUS GROUP: DRIVING BETTER PERFORMANCE

Having won the prestigious World Class Manufacturing Award of the Year in 2005, sportscar company the Lotus Group wanted to up-skill its workforce in order to drive innovation and business improvement, and maintain and sustain its world-class performance.

"Our production system is not automated and our products are hand built: to stay at the forefront of world-class manufacturing, we recognised that we would need to continuously up-skill our workforce," says John Vigar, continuous improvement and business co-ordination manager. "If we had robots we probably wouldn't hesitate to upgrade their 'software programmes'. With people, we must continue to upgrade their knowledge, understanding and their skills."

A training programme targeting 300 employees was established between Lotus Cars and City College, and made possible via Train to Gain funding. Training is delivered in house by a team of Lotus trainers, monitored by the National Skills Academy for Manufacturing, formerly the Automotive Academy, and City College. Lotus employees worked towards an NVQ in Business Improvement Techniques (BIT), focusing on areas such as safety, effective team-working, continuous improvement, workplace organisation and problem solving.

Says Vigar: "The dream of all companies is to have a problem-solving workforce, and that has been a key part of the training. Innovation, to us, is not simply about coming up with the next big idea, but having a team of people who can put their heads together and come up with a better way of doing some of the everyday aspects of our operations."

TAILOR MADE SYSTEMS: TAPPING INTO STUDENT TALENT

Warwick-based Tailor Made Systems (TMS) specialises in airfield lighting systems, including MALMS (Mobile Airfield Light Monitoring System), a mobile unit for testing airfield lighting under service conditions. The design takes into consideration system accuracy, such as the path of the vehicle, characteristics of individual light fittings and the position of measurement sensors.

In 2005, TMS was looking to extend its product range. As part of the development process, it wanted to perfect the existing model and assess how each of its functions performed.

Through the Shell Technology Enterprise Programme (STEP) the company enlisted the help of David Hewett, a mathematics student at Warwick University, to carry out the computer modelling to produce the required data. The result was a computer simulation that enabled TMS to carry out controlled tests on its product without the need to produce a physical prototype. By simulating how MALMS operated in a number of different situations, Hewett was also able to make recommendations on how to improve the product and gave TMS the information to develop a new system configuration and open up new markets.

Managing director Vernon Taylor says: "David's project will help us develop a new system configuration that will extend our product range and provide us with strong information to incorporate in our promotional literature."

award their own qualifications enabling them to attract new employees with potential, increase motivation, employee loyalty and productivity.

The new scheme also allows employees flexibility in how they train or study, for example, whether they attend an in-house or college course. It also means employees can obtain a qualification from their employer which is recognised nationally and can be used to develop their career inside and outside the company in future.

Meanwhile, Learndirect, the national 'e-learning' network, has been working in partnership with universities and colleges to launch Learning Through Work, an initiative that enables working people to achieve recognised university qualifications without taking time off, providing employers with tailored programmes of study for distinct groups of staff.

Many universities and colleges work with businesses and other organisations to operate student placement schemes, where students are matched with small to medium-size companies to work on specific projects, usually over the course of the summer. The Shell Step Placement Scheme, for example, offers resource-strapped employers undergraduate skills for a period of eight weeks. (See case study, page 33, and also chapter 4 for further details.)

It is worth noting that skills brokers, through Train to Gain, can offer a free skills assessment to anyone. They will assess what you have now and what you might need in the future; pinpointing the training that best suits your needs; selecting the most appropriate (approved) training providers, how and when the training is provided; plus which qualifications your employees will benefit from most. This includes training from NVQs to MBAs, personal coaching and mentoring. For many employers, these kinds of initiatives have resulted in major cost savings, more efficient methods, and a fresh injection of innovative ideas.

FLEXIBLE TRAINING: MEETING COMPANIES' NEEDS

Leicester College is an excellent example of innovative training provision to benefit businesses. The Train to Gain provider prides itself on offering top-quality training that fits around an employer's busy work and production schedules. Helen Keighley, head of Leicester College's Employer Engagement Hub explains: "We have a quality co-ordinator and we're constantly looking at how we deliver training effectively to reduce the time people are off the job and yet retain the quality.

"The client gets what they want in whatever way suits them. If they want employees to come into college to train we can arrange it but most of them are happier for us to send a trainer out to the workplace. "We always send our trainers out at a time that is appropriate and convenient for the employer. We have delivered a food hygiene course to a bakery in the middle of the night and even did English for Speakers of Other Languages (ESOL) training in a care home on Christmas Day. It's a question of doing what the employer needs."

Train to Gain is the simplest way for employers to address their skills shortages. Feedback from employers to the Learning and Skills Council has highlighted the need for higher level skills training across several sectors, and the expanded service now offers increased funding for Level 3 and Leadership and Management training.

Middleton Engineering is a family run business specialising in the manufacture of industrial recycling equipment. Technical director Mark Smith will be taking over the company in the near future and is therefore keen to develop his leadership and management skills.

After hearing about the leadership and management opportunities available through Train to Gain, Mark embarked on a year-long Line Management course. He was given a £1,000 grant and training was undertaken on full day and evening classes, to fit around Mark's ongoing work demands. Since training, Mark feels more confident holding company meetings and has improved his communication skills significantly.

the learning organisation

Alison Coleman looks at how directors can create a culture in which knowledge and skills are valued and shared

EXECUTIVE SUMMARY

- ☐ companies that neglect the training and development of board members do so at their peril

- ☐ the ethos of self-improvement starts at the top: directors must lead by example

- ☐ directors must ensure that the management potential of staff is properly developed

- ☐ skilled and re-skilled employees should be formally encouraged to disseminate what they've learned

The case for continuous learning, then, goes all the way to the top. Directors must lead by example and make sure their expertise and experience fit the times. If they don't, they will never be able to successfully create what's become the holy grail of HR and people management – the learning organisation.

Central to the concept of the learning organisation is the idea that the value of skills and knowledge is passed down throughout the organisation. Directors set the culture of learning and unlock the resources to deliver it to all employees – from senior and middle managers to shopfloor and junior staff.

In theory, it's all very simple, but in practice, it's often much more complex. The reality is that board members are often the last people to be considered when it comes to training and development.

the importance of leadership

Every successful business requires effective leadership to fully utilise the skills of staff. This is as important to companies that employ one or two people as it is to larger businesses.

Good leadership and motivational skills can improve your recruitment and retention. To gain loyalty and commitment you need to do more than just pay well. In a competitive job market, you also need to consider people's social and psychological needs – and this means motivating your workforce. To achieve these goals you need to:

- communicate a vision of what the business stands for and where you want it to be
- communicate values and priorities across the organisation
- ensure the work is challenging with a variety of tasks
- establish a friendly collaborative work environment
- consider more flexible working practices
- delegate tasks and allow others to take responsibility

Leading and motivating your staff helps bring about:

- higher staff retention – leading to reduced recruitment costs
- higher levels of productivity
- more innovation and creativity
- higher profits
- A better reputation – among both potential employees and suppliers

senior executive learning essential

For Dan Archer, senior researcher at the Leadership Trust's Centre for Applied Leadership Research, it's a dangerous mistake to ignore the training needs of senior executives. He argues that members of the board are often in desperate need of guidance – especially, perhaps, when they're first appointed.

"When you reach executive level, you have a much wider portfolio of responsibilities, and, for the first time, you are no longer an expert in all the fields that you are responsible for," he says. "You have to learn to let go and take a risk by empowering the people around you, and that can be quite uncomfortable.

"That is also why training and development at this level are absolutely crucial to ensuring that you fulfil your true potential."

people skills

While training in the practical, operational and legal aspects of board directorship is essential, enhancing people skills is just as important.

Mary Joyce, programme director for principals and CEOs at the Centre for Excellence in Leadership, says: "At that level, the learning focus tends to be on key issues such as corporate governance, but it is just as important for directors to have a sense of emotional dimension to their work.

"For example, within many organisations, difficult relationships, even conflict, can often exist between board members. Learning how to handle yourself and others in these situations is a valuable skill and one that is crucial to the smooth running of the company."

Similarly, those in senior management roles may be so focused on becoming more skilled in the technical aspects of their roles, such as marketing, sales and operations, that softer skills, so vital to their personal development, may be overlooked.

So what's the solution? Through formal leadership development programmes, directors from the private, public and not-for-profit sectors are working together to share experiences, learn best practice and bring new skills back to the board.

cross-border exchange of skills

Some are taking this cross-border exposure a step further by taking on leadership responsibilities outside of their paid jobs. These might include not only non-executive posts at other companies but also school governorships, working with the sector skills councils, or getting involved with a community organisation.

TOYODA GOSEI FLUID SYSTEMS: IMPROVING MANAGERS' SKILLS

Leicester-based Toyoda Gosei Fluid Systems UK is a leading manufacturer of automotive fluid handling systems.

In order to become more competitive in an increasingly difficult market, the company was forced to undergo a great deal of change.

However, because it had tended to promote from within, very capable operational staff sometimes became managers without developing the right people-management skills. Two years ago, Toyoda Gosei took the opportunity provided by the Employer Training Pilot – now the Train to Gain service – to work with South Leicestershire College's Skillspoint, a specialist workforce development team.

Skillspoint tailored its service to what Toyoda needed, analysing where training could help the company develop its business, and identifying any weaknesses in management skills. The resulting training needs assessment report recommended the training Toyoda would need to improve managerial skills, and identified the right providers.

Managing director Jeff Lee says: "Staff morale definitely improved as a result of training, and that has to mean better business results, while those taking part showed an increased enthusiasm, which was channelled into their work."

The company has also invested in the development of team leaders, and eight members of staff have embarked on the Institute of Leadership and Management (ILM) introduction to team leadership qualification.

Stepping outside their corporate comfort zone can be hugely beneficial to the individual and to their own organisation, says Joyce – as long as they have already established a good standard of leadership on their own board.

"Done in isolation, this sort of cross-border activity can be a bit hit and miss and may not deliver the full benefits if the director concerned is lacking in leadership skills within their own environment. They need to be clear about what they can contribute to another organisation, and, more importantly, what they want to get out of it."

The advice from leadership experts is to set out a leadership development plan, and spend time working with a coach, someone who can help those working at board level to reflect on how they are carrying out their role.

Archer adds: "Whether you are a senior manager or a board director, you never stop learning, and through that commitment to fulfil your own management or leadership potential, you create a learning culture that benefits everyone within the organisation, and ultimately, the business."

And what's the best way for (suitably skilled and self-improved) board directors to spread this 'culture of learning'? The answer's fairly obvious. The first step is train the next rung, the senior and middle managers and make sure they see the setting of development plans for employees as integral to their roles.

The next step is to make sure knowledge is spread. What one individual learns must be effectively passed to another. There must be a system of good communication. Directors need to encourage a culture of sharing, of

AREFCO SPECIAL PRODUCTS: DISSEMINATING LEARNING AND SKILLS

Arefco Special Products, based in Ashington, Northumberland, is a specialist mouldings manufacturer and a key supplier to the offshore industry. After breaking into the US market, the company had to increase productivity, and identified a need for training. Tapping into the Train to Gain service, Arefco put a dozen members of staff from its 40-strong workforce through NVQ Level 2 training and qualifications in plastic and rubber moulding, and approached Polymer Training, a specialist resource centre for the industry, to put a package together.

"As a small company, we couldn't take too many people away from the production process at any one time, so the flexibility of the programme was crucial," says human resources manager Dee Love.

Tuition was carried out in groups of two and three, allowing Arefco to maintain operations throughout. Staggering the training in this way brought additional benefits. Love says: "People would come back from their training and engage in discussions about it with others in the company. There was a definite sense that what was being learned was being communicated to other people, and that interaction had enhanced the training.

"We have also had team leaders coming back into work from more specialist product training and teaching other members of staff what they have learned." Since the company embarked on the training programme, it has seen changes in shop-floor attitudes.

Love adds: "We have had a very positive response from the workforce to the initiative. There is a much greater awareness of what the business wants to achieve, and people understand far better their role within that process.

"There is improved confidence, and people realise they are making a genuine contribution to our success. There is a far more pro-active approach to the way we operate, and while our productivity and waste programmes were already performing well, we have seen further improvements."

dissemination and of feedback. Such a culture can have tangible benefits. Get employees to train each other effectively and you may just save on costs – provided, of course, the rationale for that first set of training was clear.

As June Williams, a director at Investors in People, says: "Cascading training is a good way of disseminating knowledge to a lot of people within the company. However, there has to be a clear reason why the training is needed, a strategy for communicating it – how and to whom – afterwards, and a set of parameters for measuring the impact on the organisation.

"In the case of product-based training, it is relatively simple to set up a system of dissemination when the delegate returns, using traditional methods such as presentations or one-to-one feedback. If it is about people skills, it is more important to have someone else monitoring the impact."

The specifics of building a learning organisation will necessarily vary from company to company. But one thing is clear: the directors who succeed will be those who take a rigorous approach, who plan for their own and their employees' needs, who take into account every level of the business and who never forget the continuing need for self-improvement.

return on training investment

Company boards expect to see a tangible return on investment in training, says Alison Coleman

With skills gaps and skill shortages impacting on all areas of industry, directors must show ongoing investment in staff training and development, but they must also demonstrate a decent return on investment to the board – particularly if trading conditions are tough.

EXECUTIVE SUMMARY

☐ there needs to be systems in place to measure return on investment

☐ different time periods can be used as a basis for calculating ROI, but the key is to set clear parameters

☐ ROI is not always deliverable in pure financial terms, but is demonstrated indirectly through reduced absenteeism and improved staff retention

ongoing investment

Some of the UK's most successful business leaders have demonstrated an upfront, public commitment to ongoing investment – and built a solid business case to back it up. The DfES Workforce Training in England 2006 research showed that:

☐ six out of 10 employers who trained had experienced improved productivity

☐ five in 10 who trained had seen an increase in sales turnover

☐ four in 10 who train had seen improved staff retention

Duncan Bannatyne, star of the BBC's Dragons' Den television series and a major regional and national employer, recently made the Skills Pledge, which sets out to improve the skills of the workforce and make the nation more competitive and profitable.

As chairman of the Bannatyne Group, he employs 2,500 people nationwide and is a strong advocate of individual skills development within the workforce.

spreading the benefit of skills development

In particular, Bannatyne's health club business offers a wage incentive programme to members of fitness staff who learn new skills that will benefit club members. In making the Skills Pledge he has committed to increasing the number of people in his organisation with a minimum NVQ Level 2 qualification.

Chief executive of Tesco Sir Terry Leahy is another advocate of investment in staff development and has often talked about training providing a return to the organisation. He also recently made the Skills Pledge at a National Employer Service conference.

measuring return on investment

Determining the value of staff training has become the Holy Grail for every organisation, but recognising the link between investing in staff development and the bottom line is only part of the picture. As with any business investment, organisations must be able to justify what they spend by having a system in place that measures the return on that investment – the ROI. This is the percentage return that an employer makes over a specified period of time as a result of investing in a training scheme or initiative.

As the benefits of staff training to the organisation are likely to continue beyond the actual training event, it is important to identify the period from the outset as this is directly linked to the ROI figure obtained. This could be a period that correlates with the business planning time frame, perhaps a year or two years.

It may be possible to calculate a longer-term ROI, possibly for the full lifetime of the benefit, but this will depend on how long the employees who have been trained remain with the organisation and utilise the skills they have acquired.

Other employers prefer to calculate the payback period, which is the length of time it takes for the benefits of staff training and development to match or exceed the actual investment costs.

setting the parameters

Given the fact that training can encompass a broad range of business areas – from the more measurable technical and operational areas, to the less tangible softer skill areas of communication and customer care – the ability to produce exact figures to determine the ROI can seem complex and inexact. The key, then, to establishing any system of measurement lies in setting out the parameters that you are looking to see improvement in.

SWIZZELS MATLOW: SKILLS TRAINING LEADS TO SWEET SUCCESS

Well-known Derbyshire sweet manufacturer Swizzels Matlow is helping its staff learn to love their jobs, having trained two thirds of the firms 600 employees with help from the University of Derby Buxton and the Train to Gain service.

The company, which produces cult favourites including Lovehearts, Rainbow Drops, Drumstick Lollies and Palma Violets, has now trained 450 of its employees to NVQ Level 2 in Food and Drink. As a result, more of them are staying put, which has resulted in a cut in costs and an increase in productivity and profits.

"Since our training initiative began we have seen a dramatic reduction in the staff turnover resulting in an increase in both productivity and efficiency," says training and development manager Tony Salt. "In financial terms, this has helped to boost company profits by about £60,000 a year."

Because the training has been flexible, it has not impacted on production time – essential for any manufacturing business.

"The University of Derby Buxton provide an excellent course and that has been key for us. It gives staff the chance to learn about safe working practices and the specific safety standards for the industry. They then have the chance to do optional units relevant to their role, which they'll choose with their tutor."

Beverley Warhurst, an employee at Swizzels Matlow who has completed an NVQ Level 2 in Food and Drink, said: "It is great to be able to get training for the job we do on a daily basis and get a qualification for our skills. It really helps to improve your confidence and skills. The company has always encouraged its staff to learn new skills and push themselves."

AA SECURITY: WELL-TRAINED STAFF TAKE FIRM TO NEW HEIGHTS

Essex-based AA Security was founded in 1994, and although initially very successful, it faced growing competition in the security sector – an industry characterised by low margins and high staff turnover.

In 2001, managing director Wilson Chowdhry recognised that the business needed to address some fundamental issues, and that his own knowledge of management procedures and planning was limited. Chowdhry contacted his local Learning and Skills Council and Business Link for help and advice and was introduced to the Investors in People Standard.

The company achieved IiP status in 2002, which provided the prestige of recognition, and the processes and structures to bring about the changes that the business needed.

Initially the company had provided all security staff with an introductory three-day training programme and a one-day conflict management course. However, since 2004 each new employee undertakes an in-depth professional development programme, including the City and Guilds Professional Security Officer NVQ level 2. In addition, all supervisors are trained to SITO Security Supervisors standards.

Further training initiatives included giving all staff the opportunity to complete the ECDL (European Computer Driving Licence).

As the company expanded and the volume of training required became increasingly expensive, management took the decision to develop its own Training Academy, now recognised for delivering SITO and City and Guilds qualifications.

This has provided the company with the flexibility to fulfil its own training requirements, and an opportunity to diversify by providing training services for other companies in the sector, thus becoming a profit centre in its own right.

The adoption of Investors in People and the investment in training has reaped significant benefits for A A Security, with a rise in turnover from £615,000 in 2002 to £2.2m in 2007, and in gross profit from £58,000 to £363,000.

In the same period, staff turnover fell from 12 per cent to nine per cent in 2007 and customer satisfaction with staff knowledge and performance rose from 55 per cent to 93 per cent.

Wilson believes that it is the high quality of his staff that has won them new blue chip clients, such as BP Connect and the Arcadia Group, and helped them to secure two major competitive tenders from the Official Journal of the European Community. This has underlined the success of their USP and marked a new departure for the company.

June Williams, director of quality at Investors in People UK, says: "Some areas of training will obviously be easier to measure than others. A sales company, for example, will want to attract new customers while hanging onto its existing ones. They introduce a new product, train their staff to understand the product and sell it, and simply monitor the sales figures to see how effective that training has been."

Other areas of training, for example, interpersonal skills, and to a degree, management skills, can be evaluated by analysing feedback using methods such as 360-degree feedback, and employee surveys.

calculating the value of soft skills

However, it is often the softer skills that prove most difficult to assess in terms of their value to the business as a whole. "This is one area where Investors in People can be hugely beneficial," says Williams. "Working towards IiP status involves setting goals, creating a strategy to achieve those goals, and establishing a mechanism for providing feedback at various stages along the way to reaching your target."

ROI can also take several forms. While investment in staff training in sales or technical areas may reflect a clear financial return for the company in terms of increased profits or turnover, other types of training may deliver benefits that are not quite as easy to translate into financial terms.

For example, the value of learning and development in recruitment and retention skills can be measured by looking for improvements in staff turnover figures and assessing the cost savings made. Similarly, the success of a course that trains managers to conduct return-to-work interviews can be measured by virtue of any reduction in sickness absence levels over the course of a year or two years, and the cost benefits that brings.

Work-based training that leads to vocational qualifications such as NVQs, can in itself, serve as a tool for monitoring progress and performance.

universal challenge

June Williams concludes: "In today's business world, a return on training investment is critical. Companies are finally waking up to the fact that people really are their greatest asset, and if they don't invest in them properly, those people will simply move on to find an employer who will. This is the challenge facing all organisations."

LYRECO: WELL-TRAINED STAFF TAKE FIRM TO NEW HEIGHTS

Lyreco UK, part of the Lyreco Group, a global leader in the distribution of office supplies, delivers over 55,000 customer orders every day throughout the UK and holds a Royal Warrant.

However, Lyreco's management felt that in terms of having a co-ordinated people management strategy the business had begun to drift. With a large number of home workers as well as hundreds of delivery drivers working away from base, getting this right was paramount.

Training director Ian Lawson described it as being 'like a jigsaw, but with missing pieces.' "We felt Investors in People could offer us a framework and help us identify the gaps when it came to getting the best from people," he says. "In some cases we were blissfully ignorant and we needed that framework to give us clear standards of best practice."

The company wanted to address the key issues and identify its weaknesses in terms of people management. It soon realised it needed to change its business approach from regarding its staff purely in cost terms to adopting an investment-based people strategy.

The move would potentially provide a massive cost saving. Previous practice had always been to go to the open market for senior positions, which could cost up to £10,000 to recruit each manager. Promoting from within would avoid much of this cost.

The company had also been heavily affected by vast numbers of new people coming into the business and their natural tendency to make mistakes, simply because they were new to the business. This led to general dissatisfaction and a significant level of staff turnover.

Lyreco set out to create a new culture of learning. Employees are now put through trainee programmes and work experience, and the company is committed to a Skills for Growth programme.

Since changing its people development strategy and investing in training and development the company has enjoyed a 16 per cent reduction in staff turnover, and seen ten members of the UK team move into director or managing director positions in the last five years. Syas Ian Lawson: "Investors in People has made us think and made us change. We now plan and prepare beforehand. We are focused on the objectives of the event and the change in behaviour and business results we want to see and achieve afterwards. We are now much more into return on investment."

KESSLERS INTERNATIONAL LTD: APPRENTICES REAP REWARDS

Kesslers International Ltd. is an East London based company employing 250 people in a multi-skilled, ethnically diverse workforce, including 14 apprentices. The company specialises in the design and manufacture of point-of-purchase display units for major brands, retailers and information providers. Currently it is one of London's largest manufacturing companies.

Apprenticeships meet the company's specific needs. By working with external training providers Kesslers is able, as a medium sized business working in a diverse number of areas, to make sure their knowledge is up to date. Apprenticeships have also given Kesslers a longer term benefit: over the five years it has been running, it has supplied the next generation of shift managers and supplemented an ageing workforce by bringing in younger skilled people.

Since introducing Apprenticeships Kesslers has seen a dramatic improvement in speed of response and customer service, higher employee satisfaction plus apprentices tend to progress into the ranks of junior management faster than the majority of the work force. Since the apprentice mix is also multi ethnic, the effect of this has been that the company has a more diverse middle management than they had previously, approximately 10 per cent.

CHAPTER 10

2020 vision

> **Britain's top businesses increasingly see skills development as the way to secure their long-term future. Peter Bartram explains why**

The most enduringly successful companies are those that look not just at the skills they need today – but those they must acquire in the future in order to stay competitive. The year 2020 may seem far off, but successful businesses – such as global players like BT and Rolls Royce – already have an eye on the skills they will need by then to keep themselves at the top of their fields.

Like the rest of British business, they face a daunting skills challenge. The Leitch Review of Skills, published at the end of 2006, recommended that by 2020:

- 95 per cent of the workforce should be functionally literate and numerate

- at least 90 per cent should be educated to Level 2 (equivalent to five good GCSE passes)

- at least 40 per cent of all adults should have a higher education qualification at Level 4 and above

EXECUTIVE SUMMARY

- the Leitch Review of Skills set ambitious targets for the British workforce for 2020

- new working practices, new competitors and new technologies demand ongoing reviews of the skills base

- organisations must consider the HR implications of strategic planning decisions

- the induction process has a long-term effect on employees: companies must get it right

Given there are currently an estimated five million illiterate adults in the UK, these seem ambitious targets indeed. But Leitch warned that missing them will seriously undermine our ability to compete in the global marketplace – and therefore our economic prosperity.

However a recent LSC/DIUS and SSDA survey conducted on employers (National Employer Skills Survey 2007) found that there has been an increase in the proportion and numbers of employers providing training: 67 per cent had funded or arranged training for staff in the last 12 months compared with 65 per cent in 2005.

Encouragingly the percentage of employers with a training plan has also grown and is now 48 per cent (compared to 45 per cent in 2005). The percentage with a training budget has also increased. Finally, employer training spend (including trainee wages) has increased to £38.6bn, which is a 15.9 per cent increase from 2005.

raising the bar

Directors' perspective on the Leitch recommendations will obviously vary from organisation to organisation. While many businesses struggle to improve the skills of their workforces in line with them, others are raising the bar even higher

Ged Leahy, director of strategic skills and workforce planning at Rolls Royce, says the targets are not enough for his company. "We have to exceed them," he adds. "In our environment, basic skills are way beyond what Leitch describes. In our factory, our entry point is around Level 3 and, among the office population, we'd be talking about Level 4 skills."

Rolls Royce has traditionally used two capability development boards – one for management and professional staff, the other for general skills – in order to plan future skills needs. "They assess what the businesses are looking for and what skills we will need in order to produce our products and services. It's a fairly robust process and it enables us to plan what we need year on year."

strategic workforce planning

Now, however, Rolls Royce is moving beyond that approach into strategic workforce planning. It will be critical in ensuring the company has the skills it needs to stay at the top of the aerospace industry as it approaches 2020, says Leahy.

"A strategic workforce planning process is a business planning process. It has to be fundamentally linked to the business strategy and to the business plan so that workforce planning doesn't become something after the event. Instead, it becomes an integral part of that whole business strategy.

"We have already tested the approach, and it is being piloted in a number of our businesses," he adds.

In essence, the whole process means bringing workforce planning much closer to business planning – in other words, aligning it with overall strategy. Managers work with a template that enables them to assess the likely impact of a range of external and internal factors on the strategy and its workforce implications.

But Leahy notes that companies that adopt this approach also need to know much more about the existing skills of their staff than is often the case.

Rolls Royce is a company that has always treated training and skills improvement seriously. It has its own learning and development centre, which also includes an apprentices' workshop. Leahy sees much of the new training requirement being handled through this centre, although some of the management and leadership development may be provided in conjunction with universities.

"We will always be looking at where we are adding value. It is one of reasons for the strategic workforce planning," he adds.

shaping your future workforce

David Way, director of skills at the Learning and Skills Council, notes that the shape of the workforce will change significantly between now and 2020. "The number of unskilled or low skilled jobs available is going to fall from about 3.5 million to around 600,000," he says. "Those people are almost certainly in work already so they could be sitting in jobs that will disappear unless they upskill themselves."

More generally, he says the assumptions that many directors have about the baseline of skills they need to run their companies successfully will change perceptibly during the next 12 years. "You need to look regularly at your business direction and the skills you will need to support that growth," he says. He adds that, although nobody can predict the future precisely, it's clear that most businesses will need a workforce with better and different skills. Hence, the design of the Diploma which engages employers in delivery to ensure the currency and responsiveness of learning; and the government's desire to see all young people by 2015 in some form of learning or training up to the age of 18.

an inclusive approach

"Employers need to look at the needs of the whole of their workforce, not just the few. All our research suggests that if you are not careful, it tends to be the same few who get all of the focus for training," says Way. "Often, they're the people who are positive and are pretty well trained themselves.

"I think employers need to develop strategies and plans for an inclusive approach to training. I am not suggesting that every single person needs training, but I do think that employers should think about the needs of every person."

Because 2020 seems a long way off, directors need some milestones to mark the fact that they're making the progress they should. One of these could be conducting an initial skills analysis (see chapter 3) to determine what new skills their business will need. Another could be developing relationships with the people who are going to provide the key training. Yet a third could be identifying the priority staff who will drive the business forward and then mapping out what further training they should receive.

the importance of inductions

One issue that Way recommends directors should look closely at is the induction process. "Induction arrangements for new staff say a lot about a business. If people with real talent join a business and are poorly received – and get no sense that they are going to be developed – then they may well move on," he cautions.

Even so, Way warns companies against any misconception that they can simply recruit themselves out of a skills shortage in the future. "We need to train ourselves out of a skills shortage."

And he has a sharp message for those companies that don't train staff for fear that they will take their new qualifications and move to a better job elsewhere. "What is worse than training somebody and they leave is not training somebody and they stay," he says.

LEP incorporates measures with an emphasis on induction and the use of Sector Employment Toolkits will ensure a strong focus on preparation for work in general and the employer's business in particular. Pre-employment training, supported by mentoring, is a particularly effective way of ensuring people new to an employer immediately feel valued and supported in making the move from welfare into work.

widening the skills range

But many major companies, such as international telecommunications giant BT, have a clear vision of how they need to develop staff skills as they move towards 2020. "I think the organisation will be very intensely customer focused but more like a software services company than a traditional telecommunications company," says Andrew Palmer, BT's head of skills development.

As a company, BT's focus will change, and the skills of the staff will have to keep up. For example, BT needs a large number of staff with high-level technical skills. But, in the future, more of those staff will need to broaden their skill-sets to include things such as project management, customer services and business management.

Even call centre staff will need to widen their skills range. "If you look at the contact centre operation, operatives are going to have to be much more of a universal adviser in the future," Palmer says.

BT has a learning group, a central function that sets skills and training strategy. The group works with Accenture Learning, BT's learning partner, which is responsible for the design and delivery of much of the training. "The process is very much about taking a high-level view of the business's opportunities in the future, and then embedding them in the lines of business to make learning a reality," says Palmer.

He is in no doubt about the importance of developing skills in maintaining BT's ability to compete in world markets. "It will give us a workforce that is much more agile and able to respond to the customer more effectively," he says.

the big picture

There is no doubt that the nation's skills challenge is a daunting one. New working practices, new technologies and ever-increasing international competition demand an ongoing review of the skills base at national, regional and local levels.

Among the many proposals put forward in Leitch's 2006 review of skills it was recommended that by 2020:

- ☐ 95 per cent of the workforce should be functionally literate
- ☐ at least 90 per cent of the workforce should be educated to Level 2 (equivalent to 5 good GCSE passes)
- ☐ at least 40 per cent of all adults should have a higher education qualification at Level 4 and above

Leitch warned that urgent collective action was required to meet these ambitious targets and others. Failure to do so would seriously undermine our ability to compete in the global marketplace and damage Britain's chances of social and economic success in the 21st century.

However, as the case studies and service descriptions within this guide have illustrated the challenge is being tackled head on by government, business and the education and skills sectors working in partnership. The economic and social prizes for doing so are great. It is estimated that by 2020, Britain's economy could be boosted by 15 per cent and employment by 10 per cent. The net benefit to the economy may be a rise of as much as £80bn of Gross Domestic Product.

The most enduringly successful companies already understand the imperative of investment in people and their skills. Many of them have already made the Skills Pledge and benefited from services delivered by the Learning and Skills Council such as Train to Gain. These employers are looking not just at the skills they need today but at those they must acquire in the future in order to stay competitive and to flourish in an ever-changing global economic environment.

Train to Gain & Skills Pledge

To access the full range of support available through Train to Gain and to obtain advice about making the Skills Pledge please call 0800 015 55 45 or visit www.traintogain.gov.uk .

Apprenticeships

To access the full range of support offered by the Apprenticeships programme call 08000 150 400 or visit www.apprenticeships.org.uk .

National Employer Service

If you have more than 5,000 employees the Learning and Skills Council's National Employer Service can help you access training support. For information call 0845 019 4170 or visit www.nes.lsc.gov.uk .

National Skills Academies

To find out more about the network of National Skills Academies call 08450 194 170 or visit www.nationalskillsacademy.co.uk .

Local Employment Partnerships

To explore the ways that Local Employment Partnerships could work for your business and make a difference to your community call 0845 600 8192 or visit www.jobcentreplus.gov.uk/up .

New Standard

To find the best organisations delivering training and development solutions to employers call 0845 225 1310 or visit www.newstandard.co.uk .

Get On Campaign

For information about basic literacy and numeracy courses call 0800 66 0800.

Sector Skills Councils

To find the SSC for your sector or to contact the SSC visit www.skillsforbusiness.biz .

UK Commission for Employment and Skills

For more information on the UK Commission for Employment and Skills visit www.ukces.org.uk .

Qualifications and Curriculum Authority

To find out more about building a world class education and training framework, and to seek accreditation for your own in-house training call 020 7509 5555 or visit www.qca.org.uk .

Diplomas

www.direct.gov.uk/diplomas .

Investors in People

To find out more about how to improve your business through your people call 020 7467 1900 or visit www.investorsinpeople.co.uk .

Business Link

To access a range of practical advice for businesses call at 0845 600 9 006 or visit www.businesslink.gov.uk .

Shell Step

If you wish to consider taking on a Shell Step student call 0870 036 5450 or visit www.step.org.uk .

Learndirect

Learndirect Business provides online and work-based training to help companies develop and become more efficient. For further information visit www.learndirect.co.uk .

Union Learning Fund

Provides unions with access to funding. For further information visit www.unionlearningfund.org.uk .

Centre for Excellence in Leadership

www.centreforexcellence.org.uk .

Chartered Management Institute

To find out about raising business performance through management development visit www.managers.org.uk .

Association of Learning Providers

www.learningproviders.org.uk .

Association of Colleges

www.aoc.co.uk .